I0766125

THE IMMIGRANT MAP

Title: The Immigrant Map
@ 2019 Graciela Nemer Pelliza
ISBN: 9781698489636

Immigrant*s*

Albert J. Grace

Foreword

In this book, we will remove the deep sands of the concept of emigrating. Change of place, change of location, change of house, is to produce an "other world."

People, in general, underestimate the concept of travel, I intend to show that it is not the trip but how it travels.

For the alchemists of antiquity, the transmutation of matter is possible, in their texts, they reflect how eagerly they experienced to achieve the philosopher's stone, which turned everything gold; They also sought the elixir of eternal life. They are no longer here, proof that they did not find him. But I think that here we must interpret everything in its symbolism. The alchemist talked about "travel," about "changes." We were assured that everything changes when moving, when a material is placed next to another, or when separated from it, everything is and lets be depending on where it is located.

Great discovery, especially in the field of spiritual learning.

An internal transition of great magnitude that the person experiences when moving away from harmful elements for his spirit (from actions to thoughts) and when approaching the greatest and perfect, I call God.

Let's travel together in a revolution from our slime of every thought to what we see physically, walk to the top of the sky.

Sitting on a chair, defeated on a bed, nothing is learned. The sun awaits the steps; the journey begins even if we don't feel like starting it.

We left this life having learned so little, but from what is relevant that we learn and take away, that is the excellent alchemy and the passing of gold from hands to hands.

Instead of imagining what you want to do in 10 years when you are older, believe that, right now, you are ten years older, that you are that I of your future. In front of you, your adult, the young self, novice. What advice would you give yourself? What plans would you have? What is it that you would like to do today, which you would not regret ten years later?

Think about the future from the past. This is the first advice made by me for me. From my future self to my present self.

Irony may be put for the first time on the side of the good and those actions that help save their worlds.

My mother is a person with character and a lot of personality. I admire that woman very much, and I thought of her in those moments: "She never tires of being right."

Emigrate: Knowing myself. A journey of external and internal discovery and thus began this journey.

At that moment, I began to humbly transmit writing my advice, my dreams, my nightmares, and my vision of the universe, if they were valid and if they could serve someone.

He longed to acquire wisdom. Find and find unwavering faith, strength, courage, and begin to accept me as I am.

I have a circle of good people around whom I hear and trust; it is a great advantage. The same will happen to them concerning me. We work to increase the capacity for learning, dialogue, and reflection in the search for real knowledge, trying above all to reconcile spiritual reason and practice.

Among my friends, reader, you are. You always were. Now I just let you know. It is as if I were a little pot, blue, with its foam, and you, walking on a sidewalk in a big city, I tell you, with my face of water: you were always the sea. You would like to know more. I also seek to hear from you.

This work is based on real facts from immigrant experiences. Women and men who defeated fear. We have to get carried away by the hands of the Great Alchemist to transmute his matter: on a trip. The movement produces the change.

This is the certainty: we are the same, the same, the same. Here there are only mirrors in the air. If we are together today, it is because we want a collective experience, there is something I must learn or something I must collaborate on.

I have emigrated from my country for more than 17 years. Many things have happened: diverse experiences and situations of all kinds, new jobs, integration into groups or leaving others, and in the end, everything is the same: our reality.

Today, looking back, I reflect.

It would have helped me a lot to have a guide on this lonely trip, away from family, friends, my customs, my comfort zone. Stop doing more to do much better. Learn to enjoy the company itself.

Evoking people who, like me, are thinking of emigrating, are emigrating or are beginning the process, I have decided to write this guide for immigrants with the help of this story.

In an attempt to avoid generating unnecessary suffering and always remember that compassion begins with ourselves.

Migrating gives you the freedom to be who you really would like to be. Live the inner life not lived, love the work you do, have patience, act despite doubts with love, and find the shadow itself reflected in the bottom of the sea.

Migrants seek an opportunity to live a life that is worth living. With hope, the motto is to fight to the end without ever losing sight of the essential things.

Envy is an extreme version of admiration. Everyone will tell you what to do and what not to do, but the choice is always a personal and exclusive responsibility.

It doesn't matter if you emigrate with savings or not; if you belong to the middle class, for the new country, you are an immigrant.

For the brave emigrant, all his weaknesses are strengths. Walk

Have an action plan. Do things in a certain way to reach dream goals.

I think of people who want to emigrate, and I wonder: "Will they travel alone? Will they go with a family? Have work? Have money? Have friends in the new country?"

All are challenges, overcoming them involves great learning.

I write and share my life experiences to help anyone who wants to overcome the changes humbly.

In battles, not everything is achieved by fighting.

Over time you discover that to resist, many times is to win.

Migration gives you the freedom to be who you really would like to be.

Discovering a new world is an incredible feeling.
The experience of being an immigrant can only be shared.

INDEX

Foreword	1
Discovering a new world	6
Must emigrate	13
Blame	15
The fear	17
Travel Plan	20
The doubt	24
Strengths	27
Reflection	30
Freedom	33
Self-improvement	35
THE POWER OF SUCCESS	38
Author's Words	43
Introduction	48
Part One	53
Chapter 1	54
Activity One: Controlling the Thoughts	60
Chapter Two	70
Part Two	74
Chapter Three	75
Second Activity: Massive Action Plan	79
Chapter 4	92
Part Three	102

Chapter 5 103
Third Activity: Comparative Table 118
Chapter 6 126

Epilogue 161

Thanks 167

Discovering a new world

Is an incredible sensation!

The experience of being an immigrant can only be shared or lived.

Whether for bravery or unconsciousness, deciding to emigrate from your home country means facing a significant obstacle: fear.

Knowledge makes us free; ignorance fills us with fears. Immigrants are afraid. However, there is an energy that drives them to overcome that fear: that brings with them the illusion of patenting a dream in reality.

The call to a new life. Feel the request; at any moment in life, you feel as if you are going through a ray from the hair to the feet that tells you to move, and you can choose to do it or not. It is difficult to differentiate which intuition contains heart and reason and which one I only desire without a real basis of constructive action.

One day my father told us: «I am the son of immigrants. I am the father of an immigrant ». There may be immigrant families. They carry in their genetic memory the great images of movements, valleys, tundras, valleys, skies of many colors for the trip that does not stop until the distant settlement of what is already known and which is now the distant, the old; in the new settlement the opportunity, the unknown and the adventure; Is it, in short, a challenge to destiny?

Whether for study, for work, for love, emigrating can be something temporary, just for some time. Or definitive.

In all cases, the immigrant's feelings are conflicting and contradictory. They oscillate between the euphoric emotion of discovering a new world and the sense of anguish, loneliness, and sadness characteristic of uprooting. One day dawns sunny and happy, but the next black, cloudy, and dizzy.

Doubts arise without looking for them: why emigrate?

In every country, there are rich and poor. Successful and unsuccessful.

Do immigrants know why they emigrate? Why? Is it to achieve objective goals or individual goals?

(We question this in a voluntary migrant, who can decide. Of course, today, thousands, millions of mandatory migrants flee their countries because of hunger and wars.)

They ask themselves again and again: what drives me to march? What keeps me from not doing it? Will I go alone or accompanied? Why go? What factors do I have in my favor? –Work, family, friends, savings, the possibility of personal and family development– ?, Is it an option to return to my country ?, Will I set a period to assess whether to return or not?

I think that being clear about the objectives of such a radical change project is fundamental. Write it in detail and read it to make the changes that are deemed necessary to remain excited. Stay energized and motivated.

If the objectives are lost sight of, the path is lost, and what I call the "dolce far niente" falls.

In "the sweet nothing," thoughts wander from one extreme to another, lost between two worlds, between two countries without doing anything here, without doing anything there. Living day by day, passing the years and getting older, surrounded and in the middle of a vacuum, that every hour increases thousands of kilometers.

When I emigrated, I managed to set my goals after asking myself the following questions:

1. What will I do while living in a new country?
2. What does it mean to live in a new country? For example, learn another language, expand a business, meet new cultures, travel, and learn more cities.
3. How do I hope to feel in the new country?
4. How long will it take to achieve my goal?
5. What will contribute to my life to achieve that goal?
7. What will happen to family and friends? How will I maintain a relationship with them?

The affirmations also arise suddenly, like outbreaks in spring, like great truths and little lies: «How good to go, how bad to go, I will do this there that I don't do here, better not to leave because what I believe is there here; I better leave because what I dream here is surely not ».

Contradictions, certainties, doubts, like the nest of stars and constellations at night.

Migrating is a path that begins with a step. And the great phrase of The Longest Elder starts by taking the first step; it must appear here. One truth: the immigrant country is always considered a foreigner.

The reception is different for the one who has a family that receives it than for the one who arrives as an orphan.

Likewise, immigrants can identify with the new country. To think that it is their place, where they like to be, or they may not find tranquility, peace in the new place ever. There will be people who receive them well and others who do not.

The immigrant is aware that you cannot win in all battles, that everyone will not accept you and that failures are part of life.

That the smile never fails in every trip.

Not even a good mood. Whatever happens.

A tour can be a battle, but not war. Some people are intrigued to meet new, different, foreign people and invite them to participate in their lives. When these fraternal people discover that this new being full of questions is the right person, they invite him to stay.

The migrant knows that there are differences that open doors, and recognizing those differences in his favor is one of his virtues.

The changes considered help to feel stability in the face of unknown situations, and the unknown will appear every day in the immigrant's life. He knows how to recognize the crisis as the opportunity for something better to enter his life.

Anticipating a crisis forces us to challenge intelligence and improve. It is essential to be constant, even if things go slowly.

Foreigners are citizens of the world who, in certain circumstances, permanently or temporarily, do not feel identified with their country of origin.

The reasons can be political, social, economic, or particular of each person.

A good plan of action for the traveler would be:

• Transform all weaknesses into strength.

• Open doors that are closed.

• Use the differences in your favor.

• Curiosity, always present.

• Know that failure is part of success.

• As athletes, learn to fall with the least possible damage.

• Get up with renewed energy, for more and better.

• Know what enriches you, what helps your growth.

Just listen to your heart, what do you know about the feelings in it?

Now, how would you feel if you lived the rest of your life in that country? How would you feel when you left? You can always return to the home country. It is a right, not an obligation.

When we return, everything is seen differently because the person who returns is never the same one who has left.

In the end, everything is a game, everything will happen, and the questions will be: "Did you like it? Did you have fun? Did you learn something? What was it?"

To face them, to face them by saying with force and courage, «this is what I am, and I am willing to die for it.

Today I know who I am, I know what I believe in, and that is all I need to know ».

You have to believe, be focused. You have dreams, protect them, and the Universe will conspire to help them happen.

Conveniently, the focus is on areas: area of money, relationships, physical, mental, and spiritual health. The effective path is the one that motivates us and the most accurate.

Here are some guidelines so you can focus on your areas and achieve the objectives:

1. Clarity is fundamental. Clarity is power. What I am going to model what I want, why I am going to do it.

2. Quality information. The best map, the best strategy for Team strength.

3. Action. Move. A massive work is convenient. Every day act focused, focused, and focused.

They tell us that we must be realistic. Humbly, I think we can create dreams from the foundations of objective reality.

Reality is what everyone sees and agrees. If he sees that it is raining here and now, no one will say otherwise, but if I say that the rain makes me feel happy, another person can say that his truth is that the rain makes him feel sad.

The objective truth is the truth for all; the subjective truth is personal.

In the outside world, I must analyze, stop, stop activities to summarize what I have learned. New thoughts are generated and repeated until they are understood.

The inner world can be summed up in the present state plus the desired state. Pay attention: what do I say? What do I think? What do I answer? What do I hear?

I keep listening to thoughts:

√ What do you see.

√ What they say.

√ What I want.

√ When I want it.

√ How many times I want it.

√ What will I do with the success achieved.

√ How it will benefit me in different areas.

√ How I will feel about it.

Equation of results.

Living a thought allows you to overcome obstacles. We are subject to life impulses looking for their expression. They always lead us to know more, to do more, and to be more. For all that, we must have more to use, to learn, and continuously improve ourselves.

Beliefs, lies or truths, basic ideological principles that were vigorously defended and are no longer useful to us today.

Clean old programming, thoughts, and words that are no longer useful to us in the new circumstances.

The will to think in a certain way, to do things in a certain way. The hardest job is to think of "the truth," regardless of appearances.

The internal dialogue is continuous and even more when everything changes vertiginously within the circumstances of the foreigner. You have to redirect the conversation to where I want and how I want to feel.

Thoughts of presence of something or thoughts of lack of something.

Write down what we say continuously because those are the deepest beliefs of the subconscious: what are you listening?

Pay attention to present thoughts: I see the opportunity, I learn how to do it, new skills arise, new personal relationships, challenges appear.

On the one hand, there are teachers, advanced people who want to help others. Every time I meet them, I will ask about what they do to have what they have (peace, love, balance, happiness), how they do it. Through these conversations, we experience the feeling that everything is closer.

The thoughts of failure are very different. We must act very differently. We say to ourselves: "I don't accept this vibration." "No, thanks." "I don't want that today."

On the other hand, there are the negative teachers that we also find along the way, but I must be clear that they are their choices, not mine. It is your internal dialogue, not mine. The loser's focus is his focus; it's not mine. We will always banish the territory of our skin to victimhood.

It is vital to get out of a lack of thinking.

I realize what he was telling me, I forgive myself, and I promise that tomorrow will be less of lack and more of presence.

The final result can be anticipated by listening to the phrases you say. You can answer the following question: where do your phrases point?

If you think about losing weight, you must have been obese before. If you become obsessed with healing, you may get sicker. If you think about work, you will work more.

Having control of thoughts allows us to live a completely positive idea, and to have a mental block of everything that is not part of that idea. Doubt, fear is recognized and discarded from thoughts.

Not listening, not seeing, not sharing anything contrary to that idea is the way to achieve our dreams. We get together with complementary people, vibrating in the same way. We create vibrating bubbles with them and us together.

Practice focused and also spaced repetition. I allow some time for the brain to become familiar with the new idea and return to repetitive thinking strongly.

As a gymnast, there are phases of muscle training, contraction, and stretching, relaxation.

Almost two decades ago, I emigrated from my country. So many things have happened. Today, looking back, I reflect.

With objective and measurable data and with subjective data that I only feel within myself, I can take stock of the chosen path.

At first, I had a guide on this lonely trip, away from family, friends, and customs. A kind girl who selflessly helped newcomers. Her name was Andy; she is no longer among us.

I bless that woman and all those people who, like her, extend the helping hand to those who do not know, but share feelings and experiences.

I remember asking him before taking the plane to Spain:

-Worth the effort?"

"The experiences cannot be explained; they can only be shared, that is something that everyone must discover, it is something personal," Andy replied.

For the immigrant, all his weaknesses are strengths. Therefore, it is essential to do things in a certain way to reach dream goals.

The dream seeker pursues "the vital impulse" that his expression desires. It is the need that leads us to know more, to do more, and to be more.

Have more to use as learning and improvement tools. The highest goal of enriching ourselves as individuals is to live more intensely and better.

Desire is the power that tries to manifest itself. Find the complete expression. That desire to have everything I can use to express the best of each person, grow and help grow who comes into contact with you. Do things a certain way.

I understood that the body is the house of the soul. I'm in my house. Home is where I am now. Being happy now with the company and in this place, helps not to live in the past or in the future.

I am going to tell you the story of an immigrant, his lights and his shadows, his path of spiritual immigrant, his physical body also walked.

Thank you all for joining you on a great trip.

Must emigrate

First, the immigrant considers accepting the beliefs of "his people," being one of them, but soon realizes that this is impossible. He is not like that and would be one of them.

Then he tries to convince his family and the people he talked to that he thinks otherwise, that they accept the differences to stay together. The others do not take that condition.

The need to seek new answers to your questions is slowly born over time. It is already decided, has no alternative, must emigrate.

There are still things to solve before leaving "his people." Meanwhile, dreams of living in a different society, with other norms, fairer, and closer to their ideal, increase the courage to leave.

Seeing the beautiful landscape of its people, it is difficult to think that you cannot live in peace. The reality is that many times the exterior landscape does not matter as much as the landscape of the thoughts of each of its inhabitants.

A beautiful nature and a measured, sensible, respectful, honest attitude with harmonious thoughts allow us to live happily. Of course, that is possible as long as the people who live in that society look like you.

Living with maladaptive people can transform an individual's life into a nightmare.

 It is foolish; it is irrational to reach dementia just for not having enough courage to abandon the known and launch into the unknown.

It is proven that until the age of 30, the person does not have bright ideas. Their beliefs are being formed. Even though the nervous system continues to develop throughout life, the essential is already marked at that age.

Young adults are already in a position to make their own decisions with all the information they have collected in their lives until that moment.

The concepts that we must take into account are the following:

The solitude of the immigrant is one of the great learning's. We must not allow loneliness to overwhelm. Learning to be well in company and alone is essential.

Create a circle of protection with people of the same beliefs. Immigrants and people who understand that situation.

Every time someone sends destructive and negative messages that lower their self-esteem or demotivation, a technique must be put into practice:

—When you feel they are speaking negatively or are telling you something that hurts you, look the other way. That thought does not enter your head. You must say to yourself that you do not accept that thought, you return it to the sender. Imagine you are a mirror, and nothing enters you; nothing hurts you. -

Blame

To live a balanced life, where all the members of a family put their grain of sand to be able to achieve a full existence, that was their desire. However, sometimes, we confuse harmony with submission. Where is the difference?

Eliminating from our lives, everything that harms us as individuals is necessary even if it means becoming an immigrant.

Hurting others is inevitable because each person perceives the world in their way, and the interpretations are personal. Accepting the "no" is difficult, but it is even more painful when the damage has not been the objective of the action.

In the search for his freedom, the immigrant finds a potent manipulation weapon: guilt.

It is suffering coupled with a feeling of drowning that leads to condemn him to a life of psychological torture.

Guilt could lead him to develop deep sadness and the inability to fight for his desire.

Predicting the future is very bold. Light and peace can defeat unnecessary confrontation.

A full life demurely contemplated the future, without pressure and harassment. We know that the situation is very complicated.

If the immigrant regrets and abandons his dream for being overcome by doubts, fear, and guilt can completely change the course of his life.

Doubt is an obstacle when it comes to taking a path in life. It is the beginning of a process that you must develop in your person. All dreams of emigrating disappear by a decision in just a moment.

It is still possible to retract, accept to stay, but it is increasingly distant.

When he decides to leave, he erases all glimpses of doubt. Your dream has already grown, and you can take your course and fend for yourself.

When a person decides to emigrate, he suffers a fear of routine changes, of his environment and his whole life, as well as fear of separation from his loved ones.

Go from a state of magical motivation to a state of magical despair.

There is an inner struggle between the things that drives you to leave, to stand firm in your decision with an unwavering will, and the things that hold you with a feeling of unease.

The nights are filled with nervousness, embarrassment, and even despair in the face of an uncertain future, an unknown world with its challenges.

It is essential to stop the affliction, the overwhelm, and the restlessness is keeping calm, remembering the mundane things of each day, and laughing at everything you can.

The best therapy for anxiety is laughter. Feeling joy, being happy, being happy is the best therapy for anxiety.

The fear

Migrating is not valid for everyone. For many people, staying in their comfort zone is essential to avoid the death of the spirit.

The uncertainty caused by moving to a new country makes it difficult to make a decision. Feelings of loss, of failure, of sinking cause some people to collapse just by imagining the situation.

Inevitably some people think about leaving, but the idea produces restlessness and anguish. Imagining that situation generates an internal conflict so high that it paralyzes them.

They discard the idea; they are used to their state, and fear is stronger than their thirst for adventure.

They firmly believe that emigrating is something very negative. Some people judge the immigrant as careless, risky, bold, and self-destructive, instead of considering him as a person different from them.

No one is certain of anything; we only know that when concern becomes exaggerated, it becomes destructive.

Fullness does not come by magic. You have to work on it every day. Well-being is brought by discipline, perseverance in building a better life. Step by step, we get further.

The effective path is motivating and accurate.

Clarity is fundamental. Clarity is the objective, to know what I am going to model, what I want and why I am going to do it. Search for quality information: the best map, the best strategy, and the strength of the team that formed Daniel and Antonio.

Some beliefs are the lies we believe, and we have to review to select which ones are worth to us and which are left in the past (thoughts, words, results). Clean old schedules, choose to work with people who vibrate together, and want to improve. Progress as a natural being that wants to grow. If done as a team, the effect is multiplied.

Think in a certain way, do things in a certain way, even if many people say otherwise. The hardest job is to think about its truth, independent of external appearances.

I encourage you to remember:

The internal dialogue is continuous. You have to direct it where you want to feel and how you want to feel. Use all the tools that I will give you positive phrases, autosuggestion, and then we can create a new reality to start enjoying a fuller life.

What are you listening to? Thoughts of presence of something or thoughts of lack of something. Write it down, write it on paper because those are the deepest beliefs of the subconscious.

Pay attention, what do we tell ourselves? Write down what you say continuously.

Dream of being happy and being here, now full, abundant. Be everything you want to be in this instant. You are having more than you ever dreamed of right now.

It's a huge challenge, to find the seed of evil thoughts hidden in your mind, open it and heal it

For immigrants, it is essential to move away from their place of origin to settle in a different one. Improving your living conditions is the only solution you have found. The anguish, anxiety, fear, frustration, and loneliness you feel in your home have no other comfort.

Cornered, the feeling of refuge in the distance is his motivation. In another country, I could progress and grow, without identity, without anyone knowing.

What would your new life like be? How would you do it to start over?

When the idea of permanently settling in the new country, settling in, and being an entrenched immigrant causes a sense of well-being and security, it is time to leave.

There are many ways to immigrate: completely alone, make the advance alone and then bring the family, or emigrate the whole family together.

The way I recommend to those who have a family is in two parts: first, the immigrant alone and then that it is located about three months later, bring the whole family.

You have to have firm ideas to avoid falling into the mental traps that make it difficult to cross obstacles that prevent you from having a happy and full life.

The mind must guide you along new paths to move towards your dreams.

Create a defense system, both negative thoughts past and present, to create a fantastic and dreamy future. Otherwise, that information could pose a significant risk to the immigrant.

It consists of a professional silence. Keeping calm in thoughts is the key to future success. The seed of fear that nested within all people should not be awakened.

His particular tendency to trust a favorable future gives him the strength to face the difficulties that will arise with good courage.

It will be persevering in its work of identifying and valuing the positive that exists in each circumstance and individual that is in the way. Its objective is to find solutions, possibilities, and advantages always, without prejudice from other people.

With his eagerness to experience the new world, he overflows positive emotion upon arriving in the new country.

Travel Plan

The journey begins a process that was already underway.

Choosing a city does not mean it will be the final one even if, if it were, it would save a lot of time, efforts, and sacrifices.

 It is convenient to choose the largest city you find, with millions of inhabitants, with many job opportunities and as many social groups as you would have ever imagined.

A city in continuous transformation that challenges your perception of life: memorize the streets, places, people. He increased his ability to pay attention and think more quickly than he does in his hometown.

Taking root in a new city is an excellent idea. The facts confirm it: new friends, a new job and challenges.

On the other hand, the customs of the people in the new city should not be annoying. They are strange, unique but, at the same time, fun, for example, theater, cinema, complete libraries of tools for intellectual growth.

The custom of enjoying life and good times is a common social practice in the first world city. It is usual for laws to match the customs of society.

Good customs are components of society that are transmitted from generation to generation. For an immigrant, adapting to this social group was very simple.

The spiritual cultivation and its intellectual faculties are fascinating.

 Studying their customs, practices, ways of being, rituals, types of dress, and behavioral norms are aspects of this culture that became their main goal.

His goal: to learn from everyone who comes into contact with him and be a wiser person.

The native society is more primitive, with little intellectual development. The social network of the people fixes thoughts and symbols in the community to perpetuate the manipulation of their men and women, trying to maintain an ignorant and manageable society.

The emigrant is the new one, the outsider.

 The support of a social group in the new country is essential. We are social beings, and the communities support their members.

A proactive immigrant community that helps growth and offers containment is positive, cheerful, organizer of events, trips, and enriching activities.

Being part of a sports group such as a football, dance, cycling, or sports center helps social integration. Being part of a sports group makes it easy to meet people and make good friends.

We must cover the educational part, work, and the social part. Have the preparation to know when to speak and when to shut up.

Develop conciliatory ability; Leave the differences aside, reach agreements easily. Try to learn to speak every day in the same way as your colleagues do.

Patience is an admirable gift. They are having the ability to endure without altering the circumstances most contrary to their beliefs, their origin, and their way of thinking.

Without being disturbed, knowing how to remove any fear, doubt or guilt. You must ensure that patience and tolerance are maintained over time.

You should never enter into a situation of tiredness, defeat, and rejection of that reality you are living. The consequences can be unimaginable: from outbreaks of violence to maladjustment.

Remember:

You are more significant than any obstacle; you are bigger than any problem; you are the solution.

Together we create a list with the motivating phrases to fill the mind with positive energy.

 Phrases that, in the beginning, are not credible, but after repeating them tirelessly for months, they end up being familiar, to the point of becoming phrases incorporated into regular vocabulary.

Finish convinced that they are real.

Most of these phrases should start with:

"I AM." It is the most enormous power of autosuggestion that exists.

Phrases are known to everyone but repeated routinely; they become a reality.

The phrases that I liked the most were:

• I am the source of my abundance.

• I am an unlimited being. I can create what I want.

• I am abundant, and I imagine abundance for everyone else.

• I am love, well-being, and happiness.

• I am joy, I know what I want, and I get it.

• I am better than I imagined.

• I am increasingly prosperous and abundant.

• I listen and trust the advice inside me.

• I follow my greatest joy.

• I honor myself in everything I do.

• I always follow a brighter path.

• I congratulate myself on many occasions.

• I forgive myself; I know that in every moment, I have done the best I have been able to do.

• I have compassion for myself.

• I am a being of light; everything that happens is the best that could happen.

• I value myself; I give thanks for my life.

• I give thanks for the path I have chosen to travel.

• I believe in the beliefs that provide me with vitality and growth.

• I believe in my destiny.

• I am the builder of my life.

• I choose my positive thoughts.

• I love to walk the path as much as to reach the goal.

• I deserve to be happy.

• I know that the universe acts perfectly, always in favor of my supreme good.

• I know that my value and worth increase with everything I do.

• I live in a world of abundance. Everything is perfect in my universe.

• I know that only good things will happen to me.

• I trust my growing abilities.

• I believe that everything comes at the right time and in the right way.

• I show love in my daily actions.

• I make and contribute to enhancing the light, beauty, and order of the universe.

• I honor my particular skills and attitudes and use them.

• I possess a wealth of valuable attitudes and talents.

• I know what I like to do, and I do it.

• I give myself permission to think and dream without limits.

• I follow my internal knowledge.

• I am a valuable person; my path is essential.

• I accept myself and love myself for what I am at every moment.

• I am a unique person.

• I permit myself to be the best I can be.

• I am committed to my path.

• I choose evolution and vitality.

- I invite good and allow you to enter my life.
- I follow the flow and stay alert to my opportunities.
- I choose to part with everything that does not serve my highest good.
- I get rid of things easily, knowing that nothing comes out of my life if it is not replaced by something better.
- I bring love and a positive attitude to everything I do.
- I create everything I want easily and effortlessly.
- I have abundant resources while on my way.
- I always give my best to all people.
- I appreciate what I am and what I have.
- I thank you for my life.
- I give from the heart. Every gift that serves and strengthens others.
- I am generous with myself.
- I serve others the best I can.
- I experience clarity and harmony in all my energy exchanges.
- I am always guided towards a superior solution.
- I always look for everyone to win.
- I have abundance in all areas of my life.
- I send others thoughts of freedom and independence.
- I choose the life I want to live in joy and abundance.
- I am a grateful person. I value all the good that I have in my life.

These are some of the many endless phrases that can whisper in your ear every day, several times to convince the mind of the immigrant.

Many days he is more reluctant to believe in his own words. Difficult days where your old beliefs do not leave your mind alone.

The doubt

Many times the mind seeks to return to its known area and in different ways, confuse the immigrant. Make him believe that he is wasting his effort, showing contempt for what he deserved esteem and respect.

When you acknowledge having let fear into your thoughts, you must start the road again with new phrases.

The experience of negative thoughts causes the desire to return to the path of positive change. We all have a tolerance for pain; when the limit is exceeded, decisions are made differently.

Recognizing that destructive thinking has entered is the most important thing to stop the negative cascade.

You must congratulate yourself on having seen it come in, and now you have to redirect it. A metaphor would be: "if a wolf has entered his house, does not face him, you redirect him to another door so that he goes outside and goes away".

The negative thoughts that come in, you can redirect with some very powerful words that you should use as many times as necessary until the wolf gets tired of entering and leaves without returning. The words then and now.

The word "then"; For example, a thought of you don't know how to do something, you are not good, that you are no good ... you already entered, you could not do anything and, without realizing it, that thought is already in your head. Do not stop there; continue the sentence saying:

"... and then I'm on my way to learn how to do it."

"... and then I'm on my way to being a better person."

«... and then today I choose to learn more and better».

"... and then today, I don't accept you in my life or my head."

The other word is also powerful. For example, come into the memory of damage you did in the past, don't stop at it, follow the thought by completing the sentence:

"... now I know what I didn't know then."

"... now I do it differently."

"... now I forgive myself and permit myself to learn."

"... now I know that I did it the way I knew it then."

"... now I know that I do it differently."

You will see how life acquires another meaning. Being kind to yourself is the first step in being able to be kind to everyone else.

Days go by; they seem to be longer than usual with so much to pay attention to. So much to learn and a new life to build.

Having the feeling of being in preschool again, learning to write, add, and subtract.

Everything learned is not valid in the new city, the firm ground became quicksand, transforming the necessary experience into a continuous challenge.

Starting over, seeing everything differently, enjoying everything, laughing, reacting happily to the circumstances.

Therapy of the laugh:

A spontaneous smile cures any bad thoughts, and the people around them too, infected by laughter, can't help laughing.

Laughing with the eyes, with the mouth, with the body in a natural way, is healthy. It is the joy of living.

The feeling of happiness and joy is felt, transmitted with words, gestures, laughs, and actions to the whole group of friends, work, or wherever you go.

Joy is the usual mood even though not all people like to see their happy fellows.

Never stop laughing. Many people would love to be able to have joy and transmit it.

Now I wonder: how is it possible that a person who has lived subjected all his childhood and youth to abuse could get ahead and start again with that joy?

How is it possible to overcome destructive beliefs, cellular memory, and unhealthy thoughts or relapse?

How is it possible to become a person totally opposed to what he had always been?

The answer is in pain.

Prayers at Mass say, "Thank you, my God, for the pain you teach so much."

The pain can be physical, with sensory and objective experiences, or it can be a mood, emotional, and subjective pain.

In humans, experiencing pain triggers various mechanisms to limit their damage. These range from the reflex act of removing one's hand if one burns, to stress, and living in a continuous alert.

There is a process of change necessary to get out of pain, and it needs all the resources of the person: physical, mental, and emotional.

Implementing physical exercises, logical and mental activities, and having the emotional support of new friends help modify the characteristics of an immigrant to adapt to the country of his new residence.

The feeling of sorrow and sorrow leads the person to maximum frustration. As my father says: "What doesn't kill you makes you stronger."

The immigrant gets stronger. He has immeasurable physical and mental power. With his actions and effort, he alters the direction, meaning, and speed of the following events in his life.

Strengths

The immigrant must overcome numerous challenges, carry out different plans and tasks without allowing anything to distract him from his goals.

Calm outwardly but unstoppable at the same time. Know how to wait and take the delays with a smile. Having a commitment to the life you have chosen and the obstacles inherent in human reality.

Patience is one of its strengths. A fundamental pillar to achieve the successes and personal assessment that you so desire, the reason you abandoned your previous life.

Dedicated to his new principles, he worked and learned from himself and his environment. Now he has freedom; he is the creator of his life. He thought in a different way, to be full of courage to achieve the most desired dreams of his youth.

Some coworkers are anxious and impulsive, but he must demonstrate committed and constant action. Consider facts and variables that could be undetectable to others.

Always keep the instincts controlled so that the situation continues to be pleasant and calm.

Action plan:

• Get a job that you like, where you value it, and can grow.

• A cozy residence with nice neighbors. No matter if it is a room, the indispensable condition is to be in the center of the city. Away from lonely and dark areas.

In the same country, each city has its style. Now; he has chosen according to his will and not by the designs of chance because he was born there.

He learned to manage money. Having liquidity is very important to have the necessary economic freedom and continue making your own decisions.

Making accounts, you need accurate information on how much you need to be able to live in the new country.

The feeling of uprooting exists and always appears. It is essential to be clear about the objectives of such a radical change project. Some people suffer at first, and others suffer when a few years have passed.

The uprooting described it as missing that feeling of "feeling at home."

It increases at night, on holidays or, suddenly, through a memory.

One way to overcome it is when you understand that the body is the house of the soul. Home is where we are now. Being happy now. With the company we have; and in this place it helps not to live in the past or in the future.

 There were times when he plans to return to his origins. Maybe because of the longing.

What drives that desire to return?

What holds you back for not doing it?

Why come back?

Is returning an option?

Have you set a time frame to assess whether or not you return?

It is necessary to write your notes to have bright ideas. Write in detail and read them to make the changes that are considered necessary to remain excited. Continue the immigrant's path with energy and motivation.

If the objectives are lost sight of, the road is lost and falls into what I have called "the pleasure of doing nothing.

The successful immigrant is able to transform all his weaknesses into strengths. Open doors that are closed for most people. He is able to use insurmountable differences in his favor.

Curiosity is always present in him. He does not give up and is aware that failure is part of success. Like athletes, if you have to hit yourself, learn to fall with the least possible damage.

Every day he rises with renewed energies for more and better.

Whether for great courage or great unconsciousness, deciding to emigrate from your home country means overcoming fear.

The brave are also afraid, but there is an energy that drives them to overcome it. The power of the illusion of making a dream come true. The call of a new life, in a place far from the circumstances that currently conspire against a full, complete, and happy life.

You can lose battles, but you are not allowed to lose the war. We know that there are differences that open doors and others close it; recognizing those differences is a virtue in their favor.

Knowledge makes us free; ignorance fills us with doubt.

In physiology, it has been studied that the mind can only grow in a zone of stability. As a plant that grows in a place, at a particular time, but cannot grow if we are continually changing its roots. It is convenient to leave the plant in the same place when you have found the right soil.

Like a plant, children and people grow when they are in the comfort zone, in the safety zone. The changes considered help to feel stability in the face of unknown situations. They call it "calculated crisis."

The unknown appears every day in the life of the immigrant. He recognizes the crisis as the opportunity for something better to enter his life. The crisis forces us to challenge intelligence and improve. It is essential to be constant, even if you go slowly.

What nourishes your roots? Just listen to the heart, what do you know about the feelings that are stored in it? Because what the tree has of flowering lives from what is buried in its roots.

Reflection

When a year or so has passed, the immigrant raises other questions.

How would you feel if you lived the rest of your life in another country? How would you feel with the experience of returning?

Every day, when the day ends, he asks:

"Did you like it? Did you have fun? What did you like most? What did you learn?"

In the way of the immigrant, there are different types of blockages: real, external, personal, beliefs, and constructive or destructive family memories.

One technique to overcome those moments of doubt and particular confusion for these circumstances is "the technique of contrast."

It is easier to make a list of what we do not want than one of what we do want.

The technique is to think about what we do not want, and the opposite is written on paper. We leave a space for the title and, once we have finished the list, we write the title "yes I want."

After answering the questions, the immigrant feels strengthened.

At the end of the exercise if you can say this phrase:

"I know who I am, I know what I believe in, and that's all I need to know."

In good time, mate. You have done it very well. You have to believe, be focused. You have dreams, protect them. The universe conspires to help you make it happen.

Discover a trade, a business, a successful job. A profession in which you are comfortable. A profitable business with a future. A job, unlike a job, allows personal growth. Employment is routine and does not allow growth.

You must have a total commitment to learning. Experiment with the person or people with whom you will learn for some time, a weekend, a week. It takes distance. Neurons accommodate new information, new nerve circuits, and back to total commitment to learning.

Spaced repetition, let the brain adapt to the new learning system like the Zen master and then return to mass action.

The information must be assimilated and, if I suddenly gave it, it would be a blow, not a help.

Every morning before starting the day, you must remember:

- Clarity is fundamental; it is power.

 What am I going to model today? What do I want? Why am I going to do it?

 Search for quality information. Person or people who know more than you. The best map The best strategy The team strength.

Remember to move. A massive action in the direction of your dreams is convenient. Every day act focused, focused.

We are subject to life impulses looking for their expression. They always lead us to know more, to do more, and to be more, for all that, we must have more to use, to learn and continuously improve ourselves.

The hardest job is to think of the truth independent of appearances. It is to choose, with the will, to think in a certain way, to do things in a certain way, very different from how it was done until that moment.

The immigrant carries beliefs without considering whether they are real or are from their country. Thoughts, words, results, you should try to clean that schedule to adapt to your new situation.

Choose to work with people who vibrate together to improve. Progress as a natural being that wants to grow. If done as a team, the effect is multiplied.

Every so often, you have to make an equation of results. A summary of what has been learned and its results.

 Every time we learn something new, new thoughts are generated and repeated 95% of the time we think.

We create habits in our outside world according to the new thoughts acquired. Our inner world (internal dialogue) generates them. Do you know what the inner world is based on? It is the present state plus the desired state.

Leaving his native country for the emigrant is to follow momentum. The vital impulse that seeks its expression. It is the need that leads him to know more, to do more, and to be more.

Have more things to use, to learn, and improve ourselves. The goal of enriching ourselves is to live more and better.

Desire is the power that tries to manifest itself. Find the complete expression. He wants to have everything you can use to express your best, grow, and help every person who comes into contact with you grow.

Do things in a certain way to get different results constantly.

Every day, it seeks information from all support centers, advice for foreigners from official, religious, or private centers.

Be part of the country's immigrant associations. Participate in social events, go to all meetings. The important thing is to have fun, enjoy everything and with all the people.

Freedom

Commitment is an obligation to give the floor and a promise with a declaration of principles.

After so many hardships, the obligations begin.

The free will that the human being has is the greatest gift of the Universe. We have total autonomy; we can choose according to our will. That is a great blessing and at the same time, a great responsibility. We must always take care of the consequences of our actions.

The family, society, and people who depend on us place their trust. There are many expectations; things are expected of us, imposed without even knowing if they co-exist with our own goals and dreams.

Very often, we have the feeling of disappointing the people around us. I am not sure if it is because we are not good enough or because we do not want the same things, the same objectives, or the same goals as our fellow human beings.

The ritual of meditation is essential always to have clear ideas. Breathe deeply and continue with personal growth.

The immigrant who has overcome all obstacles presents himself to the following challenge.

Answer the question:

What should I do now? What is the most suitable path for me?

 He has the power to decide and act on his own. It is not tied to a destination. There is nothing written in your life; will create it according to your dreams

Without conditioning, you can choose between different paths, always learning more and better. Challenges and obstacles help us stay active and awake in life. Everything comes, changes, and everything happens.

A person must create a life that is worth living and enrich his mind and spirit with experiences and then share them with the world.

The mind must be busy creating wonders. In a continuous movement, because in an idle mind, evil thoughts nest.

A wasted mind seems to be lost in the days, and the person lives without living.

If a mind is not busy building, it begins to deal with destroying. You always have to be thinking about something, so let's give something good to think about.

 That happy and cheerful child that once was can become an obsessive adult, overwhelmed by carrying out specific actions that have not even stopped to think if they are what they want or if they do well.

Some people blindly follow the orders of others, do not see the harm they do to them, and ultimately lose their freedom, joy, and love for life. It can lose the excellence of the human being, the dignity and the important actions are forgotten.

Dignity is a quality that depends on the rational. It is the person who governs himself with righteousness and honesty. You are always able to change the path of your life, change the course, improve your situation, and redirect it thanks to free will, to the exercise of that freedom that has been given to you.

That is why it is so important to overcome obstacles and challenges that cross the road. They educate us, allow the person to make their decisions based on knowledge, and making use of the fullness of their intelligence.

If someone took away their freedom, you would lose their dignity and respect. His self-esteem would be in real danger. Life in these conditions loses its meaning and purpose.

Everything happens in a moment, the whole life, but the memories last forever.

"With my freedom, today, I choose a life that is worth living. Thank you, thank you, thank you."

Self-improvement

From the earliest times, we know that man has sought physical, mental, and spiritual improvement.

We can study in books, a study in computers, and study at a desk to have knowledge, but the understanding of what is learned is only acquired with the application and with the experience.

Understanding is an essential skill in which a series of abilities, of knowledge applied to everyday life, are displayed.

We must thank the challenges, obstacles, and adversities that arise in our lives because it is the most valuable way to gain experience.

The immigrant carries his heart divided into two worlds: the world that was born and the world where he makes his living.

Where are you from, immigrant?

"I am a citizen of the world. It is formed of two parts.

A part of me is joy, peace, hope, love, serenity, empathy, generosity, compassion, faith, kindness, benevolence.

The other part is full of rage and fights continuously against the whole world. It is arrogance, guilt, self-pity, resentment, lies, false pride, superiority, ego, envy, and anger.

On some occasions, it is difficult to live with both parts in my head. They have big fights, fierce fighting because they both try to dominate my heart.

How have I survived mental disputes?

Accepting the two parts of my being and giving my attention in balance to both.

Every time I have attended more to my positive and kind part, the other hid in the shadows to jump on me every time I was distracted. Always angry and attacking.

Both have qualities. One is compassion, strength, care; it is fair and calm. It relaxes me and helps me to reflect.

I must admit that I have managed to find the qualities of my negative side. She has tenacity, has courage, is brave, with excellent strategic thinking and strong determination. Those qualities are also necessary.

By taking care of both parties, they calm down, there are no fights, they serve me well and do nothing except for something bigger and better.

I pay attention to both, and the internal struggle for my recognition disappears. In those moments, when the internal battle disappears, the mind calms down, it is possible to hear the soft voice that arises in my heart.

It is useless to live torn in a continuous internal war. Always interacting with those opposing forces within me and how I do it determines how my days are.

When I achieve peace and inner balance, "I have everything."

The Power of Success

Graciela Nemer Pelliza

Title: The Power of Success.
@ 2018 Graciela Nemer Pelliza.
Cover Illustration. Oscar Martín Antón.
1st Edition. ISBN: 9781981071760

Share your opinion:

Dedicated to my children José y Guillermo

Author's Words

In difficult situations, we need easy solutions.

When we are going through a moment of crisis, changes or frustrations, everything becomes a challenge. The slightest inconvenience becomes an immense mountain, so solutions must be simple.

The power given by success is to have inner peace, physical health, clarity of thought, both mental and emotional.

Enjoy the small and big things in life every day. How many years have you been calm, relaxed and enjoying every day?

How would you feel if you were successful in your life?

This book proposes a series of simple step by step solutions to get out of a loop of frustration, worry, and sadness.

Your complete guide to success, in everything that is proposed as a goal in life.

To succeed, to feel success is to be here, now, happy and abundant. Be everything you want to be in this exact moment... Having more than you ever dreamed of right now, at this moment.

I have been through depression. I was medicated with antidepressants and I went through psychological treatments because I did not see beyond my suffering.

It's been more than 15 years. Today, I can say that I have been awakened. I have a broad vision. I see people, I see what happens, I see everything and I understand it. When I see anguish, pain, sadness, and suffering in some people, I remember when I was in that situation. Anxiety, grief, nostalgia added to fear and guilt.

I also see love, happiness, balance, simplicity in the material and spiritual wealth of many other people.

I was not always awakened like this. There were times when my harshness of thought in combination with a lack of compassion towards myself clouded my mind.

There are many causes that lead us to these states of deficiency and honestly, they are personal. It can be loneliness, abandonment or poverty. But of course, there is also an inherited predisposition to suffer from depression. Silence full of anguish.

I remember when I walked without looking around. We become distracted; we do not participate in meetings. We are like zombies sunk in our obsessive convulsive thoughts.

In times of storm, staying afloat is already part of the victory.

During my periods of crisis, I have studied people with success, their techniques. I have created a specific formula that works. Testing it for 10 years, I wrote, practiced and perfected this technique in the professional and personal sphere and, without realizing it, I had created THE formula.

In the wheel of life, a confident person succeeds in all aspects: at home, family, socially and culturally, physically, mentally. **All in one.**

It is impossible to succeed when one of the aspects that make up the individual being is maladapted or is not in balance.

The being, the having and the doing must coexist in harmony. The feeling of fullness and balance depends on it. If you have more than what you consider acceptable to you, you will lose it; if you do more than your inner balance can withstand, you will get sick.

The various aspects that form our personality work in different ways:

The mind works in the action mode. It is used to making a decision, acting on it and seeing the result. For example, you decide to make food, you act and see the result, the effect of that action is equivalent to food being ready.

The spirit, the heart or the inner being works differently. While the spirit seeks the permanent state of being, the body is accommodating the temporary state of being.

The spirit leans towards "a permanent state of being" or "a temporary state of being". I am happy now. We make a very common mistake if we look for results after we act in the "temporary state of being". If the mind intervenes, you will feel great frustration when you become aware of the fact that there is no immediate or quick result of the action made. It is a slow process to achieve the objectives.

For the "permanent state of being" it is very discouraging when the mind interferes with its action mode and does not see the results immediately. The person ends up being confused, tired and cannot imagine that the actual solution is very simple. Identify, separate what is "permanent state of being" from the situation of "temporary state of being".

Change the way of doing things.

The current situation generates thoughts, positive or negative; everything depends on our ability to adapt to changes that are presented to us. Facing the crisis by accepting the present as it is and being firmly convinced that everything will be fine. Taking the right actions is actually what will make the difference in the final result of our goal.

When a person enters the loop of feelings of failure, of impotence, the feelings would leave momentarily. However, the monotonous daily life would make them remember it and they would return to the same negative state, from which they can't escape alone.

In those negative days, I recall a memory which was a phrase, which I clung to as to a lifesaver: "I will never lose hope that one day I will do something that will make me feel very proud".

Introduction

Every person that follows the steps, which I am going to detail in this book, will become successful and will triumph in their objective.

Sometimes, the difference between winners and losers is very obvious and sometimes it is very subtle. A change at the right time is enough for a person to transform into everything they always dreamed of being.

Success does not care that you are tall, short, beautiful, intelligent, ugly if you have a license or not.

This book should be read part by part. The order is very important; it completely alters the results if this is not followed properly. To build a house, you always start with the foundation, then the walls and at the end of the roof.

This book will instruct you to do homework, complete tests that must be filled in with conscientiousness and with sincerity, for this book to be the best guide on the way to your success. No one will read or evaluate them, they are only for you.

The first part is fundamental - designing and clearly establishing the objectives so that when you reach them, you will be fully aware that you have achieved them by applying the formula that I will detail.

Each time you have new goals you must do the steps in order, with the right intensity and at the right time.

The second part is the continuous action. As athletes, after preparing all the equipment necessary to carry out the sport, they prepare to train. The training is also fundamental to achieve the skill level. The equation - time and training - is always directly proportional. The more time you spend learning a language or playing a musical instrument, the greater your skill becomes. You need to do the activities in the way that I am going to describe, without doubting for a moment that you are on the path to success.

In the third part of the book, we appreciate the results. We assess how it has worked so far. What has been achieved, what we have to change and what remains to be achieved. Just as physical training is not the same for all people, the same goes for mental training.

In the end, in the last chapter, you will have **<u>FOUND YOUR RECIPE</u>** to achieve the goals that you have proposed at the beginning.

Every time a new challenge is proposed, you will achieve it faster. It will be more efficient because you will acquire new experience and skills in the meantime. You can reread the book, your personal notes and do the exercises, which I will detail, over and over.

You will achieve the goals in a shorter period of time and have the ability to change them according to your new situation. Your notes, your exercises, and the book together are the straight line towards your subjective and objective triumph.

Being brave and successful is a daily choice. It is a path that begins with a step. The absolute commitment.

Wake up every day with good feelings. Admire, value, be the type of person who reaches their goals.

More than 15 years ago I decided that "I can make a choice". Have an insight; make my brain work in another way. Many things have happened, new experiences, new situations, new jobs, social groups and today, looking back, I reflect:

I can make an assessment of the achievements with objective data and an assessment of the achievements that are not looked at with subjective data, those that I can only feel inside of me.

It would have helped me a lot to have a guide on that lonely road. An interior trip away from family, friends, my habits and my comfort zone, but now I have it.

Today, I think of people who, like me, are looking for how to make a change in their lives, they fight or want to start the process of change. I offer this complete guide for brave success.

I repeat, to achieve the results, I recommend moving on to the next chapter only when the tasks I propose have been completed. We need to have the written material from the previous step in order to get through the next one.

It is not a race of time; it is a process of objectives. It is not important at all if we take more time to complete one step, the important thing is to be consistent and to reach our goals. The difference in doing it in writing is fundamental.

With this method, we write our own personal map of success.

Part One

Chapter 1

Why and What for:

Being proactive means taking control of events instead of just watching things happen. Being proactive takes time since it involves considering different options, weighing possible alternatives and making your own decisions in order to achieve your goals.

Pro-activity is an attitude in which a person actively takes absolute control of their behavior. It means taking the initiative, anticipating the events, being responsible for what happens and making decisions at all times. A proactive person is able to react to any circumstance without immersing themselves in it.

A reactive person is affected by the circumstances, conditions, and the social environment. They have no control over it and react without evaluating the consequences or they become paralyzed. They may not see beyond situations and assume an attitude of denial and pessimism. They only feel good if they are inside their "comfort zone".

Psychological reactivity is a phenomenon by which individuals alter their behavior or demeanor when they suspect they are being observed. The changes that occur can be positive or negative, and depend on the situation itself.

Accepting that we are reactive or proactive people will help us in our transformation process. What for some would be a negative characteristic, we transform it into our favor.

It is fundamental to be attentive to our inner world in order to stop the stream of thoughts that arise from the head and listen to that soft voice that comes from the heart.

What do I say, what do I feel, what do I think?

We look at it as if we were watching a movie of our life.

Because there is no need to be afraid of our "light".

In this chapter, the goal is to empty our mind, so we can fill it with the thoughts of our choice. I have to discover what I think, what I say to myself in my thoughts and how I feel about it, to be able to rediscover my entire mind. The mind cannot absorb new knowledge until we empty it of the old one. It acts like a sponge. If it is full of water, it can no longer absorb.

How is a successful person like?

For people with a successful mind, all weaknesses are strengths.

The plan of action is to do things in a certain way, to reach the dreamed goals. To transform the things, which come our way, in our dreams.

The path that has led you to your experiences cannot be explained, it can only be shared.

We must acknowledge that we do not know everything. There is an <u>unconscious incompetence</u> when I do not know what I do not know. When I realize that I do not know, there is a <u>conscious incompetence</u>. I learn, I do the necessary actions and I transform, now I know what I know, there is a <u>conscious competence</u>. When it becomes a habit, I do it automatically like driving. I do not know what I know, <u>unconscious competence</u>.

Contemplation; how do we react to what happens to us?

It is important to create a stable space for us and pay attention to repetitive thoughts because everything that resists persists. What we focus on by our will or just by not realizing it, is exactly what is going to expand to our reality.

I honestly propose that we focus on objective actions and conscious or unconscious subjective actions.

Always from the point of respect and consistency.

Having coherence is to be coherent in our actions; it is a very difficult job to carry out habitually.

We need to differentiate our mental stories and the incorrect images engraved in our minds, which we got from the reality that our fellow human beings live, such as our clients, relatives, and friends. This will help us not to harm innocent people because of our current frustration.

The Goal of Success

When we talk about the power of success, we refer to being able to do what we want to do and feel fulfilled for achieving it.

For each person, the power of success means something different. For a Tibetan monk, for an athlete or for a musician it is different than for a Wall Street broker.

We need to specify what the success of your project entails.

<u>What is success for you?</u>

It has to be something measurable, for example, learning to play the guitar, learning to play a sport or achieving a standard of life for your loved ones and yourself.

The goal can never be just to have a certain amount of money, to surpass another person in their achievements or to show someone how much we are worth because none of that is enough of a motivation for so much effort put in it.

Money should be a tool to feel a certain way, another person's achievements are theirs and we will have our own and, finally, you don't need to prove anything to anyone. If they love us, they will love us as we are and if they do not love us, we cannot force them to change that either.

The goal has to have personal value. The satisfaction of speaking a language and being able to communicate at your work, helping your children, parents, others or yourself to overcome any obstacle.

To have a higher degree of physical or intellectual development in order to grow as individuals. Have the experience of being yourself but better.

Today, we know that the decisions made in the past have created the current world in which we live. The decisions we make today will influence our future.

Live the Chaos

There is a time span, between the action and the desired effects, in which a person lives in chaos. The chaos between the desire for the future and the current reality.

We are facing a situation that we do not like: anxiety, frustration, and anguish enhanced by memories. Our mind only encourages that feeling, it boosts it. To counteract this moment, I recommend developing a new skill - the ability to coexist with the frustration in a balanced way and say "Live the Chaos".

"Illusion" is the art of getting excited. Staying motivated and positive will help the course of the event. Fear destroys, but value builds.

Give yourself what you need.

Choose expansion and growth; the evolution allows us to live an experience and have the attention on the now and bodily sensations.

We are working on our habits. These habits have brought us to where we are today. The challenge is to face them, recognize them and choose to change them.

Activity One: Controlling the Thoughts

The Technique of Controlling or Accepting the Thoughts

Once I read: "the control of thought is the control of everything else, of ourselves" and I could have never imagined how important that phrase was.

Knowing what you think in order to pinpoint your thoughts allows you to understand "the why", the causes that lead you to where you are now. You need to become a spectator of a movie, without getting into your emotions and write down all the details.

We will do the work, with an attitude in which we assume full control over our behavior in a proactive manner. This implies taking initiative in the development of creative and bold actions, with the goal to generate improvements.

Exercise: 1st Calendar of Positive Thoughts

Start with a personal calendar. We take the seven days of the week and choose to start at a time (morning, afternoon or evening) on Monday, Tuesday, Wednesday, Thursday,

Friday, Saturday or Sunday with a feeling of positive energy. Without a complaint, without blaming anyone or ourselves for anything, without justifying anything.

Note down positive thoughts with a symbol (+++) in the morning, afternoon and evening.

M	T	W	T	F	S	S
						1
2	3	4	5	6	7	8
9	10	11	12	13	14	15
16	17	18	19	20	21	22
23	24	25	26	27	28	29

30	31					

The moment, in which the energy changes to negative (complaint, guilt, justification) note down the cause, image or thought that originated it. The calendar has to be restarted.

We should feel good continuously for as long as possible. At first, it may not be like that on the third day. As we continue to practice, it will happen in a week, in fifteen days or a month.

It is essential to know which thoughts cause the change in your mood; determine if it is realistic or a creation of the mind. If it is possible to change, it will change. If it is not possible to change, we accept it. 80% of the thoughts are repetitive if you discover that, you have 80% of the changes done.

When you discover the origin, anxiety may get even worse. If that is the case, physical exercise is very good: going to the gym, walking, rearranging the closet, cleaning up the desk or dancing are activities that tire and achieve the goal of distracting obsessive thinking that leads to a negative state of mind.

We need to maintain high energy, be spectators of our life. Mastering this exercise, we will be able to move to the next stage of the calendar. Choosing what you want to think about is the first step to everything else.

Data Obtained from the Calendar:

Doing the calendar will help you in many aspects of your goal.

In general terms, the conscience is defined as the knowledge a being has of itself and its environment.

When I practiced this technique, I discovered that there were times in the day, when I had to stop. When you need to recharge again, rest or have an appetizer at the right time.

I finally knew my circadian rhythm that is very personal; we are all different and the only way to discover it is to be aware of your daily life. Some people need to sleep 6 hours, others 8. Some people are more active in the morning, others at night.

The daily sleep-wake cycle allows us to organize our behavior over time and internally synchronizes the regulation of many biological processes such as the rhythm of the body temperature or the rhythm of cortisol. The hormones that partake in circadian rhythm, among others, are: growth hormone (HC), melatonin (MLT) and prolactin (PRL) induced largely by "zeitgebers" (internal or endogenous clocks).

The circadian rhythms form the human biological clock that regulates the physiological functions of the organism so that they follow a regular cycle that is repeated every 24 hours, and that matches with the states of sleep and wakefulness.

Another fact we will discover is awareness of the days in the month when we are more proactive. Within chronobiology, a biological rhythm is an oscillation of a biological parameter dependent on an endogenous clock and environmental synchronizers.

The state of being awake is a conscious state that is characterized by a high level of activity, especially in relation to the exchange of information between the subject and its environment.

We know what are the hours and days of the month that we are more aware of the actions when we are more awake and connected to reality. The state of consciousness is that, in which the higher neurocognitive functions are active.

The state of consciousness determines the perception and knowledge of the individual psychical world and the world around us.

Exercise: 2nd Calendar of Directed Thoughts.

After a month of doing the technique, we will assess how the awareness of our thoughts and their consequences has influenced our professional, work and personal development. Note down all the benefits and changes you want to work on.

The following month, we will put in the calendar a title, some motivational phrases and we will paste some images that, when seen, will remind us of those quotes.

" Sentence"				"Image"		
M	T	W	T	F	S	S
						1
2	3	4	5	6	7	8
9	10	11	12	13	14	15
16	17	18	19	20	21	22
23	24	25	26	27	28	29

30	31					

Example Phrases:

- I observe what happens every day with fairness.

- I differentiate the facts from my mental stories.

- I am free because I have nothing to take care of and I am not attached to people or objects.

- I treat every person I talk to (waitress, cashier, customer, business person) as if my life depended on them tomorrow.

- I stop controlling, I control nothing. Is it really important?

- I am a unique person and I deserve to be loved.

- I am in the process of increasing my income; I value the security that savings give me.

- I indirectly see the mistakes and correct them; I take care of what happens inside me.

- By loving myself I choose my path, I act with perseverance and discipline.

It is very easy to do but very demanding to finish, because it requires perseverance.

In the previous calendar, you noted down (+++) on days that you remained focused on your thoughts. When you are distracted from the focus, you should note down on what day and for what reason you did not keep it up. Start with the calendar again.

We will investigate the calendar of positive thoughts and annotations. The list of positive thoughts we have had. We will call it: optimistic, happy, joyful, and proactive.

Then we make a list of our negative thoughts. What will you call it? Fear, Anxiety, Sadness or Guilt? The goal is to locate the deep roots of what you are experiencing, without any judgment.

The meticulous study of every single day will tell us what are the habits of actions, images or thoughts that take us away from our chosen phrase. Don't be discouraged, it will take us two to six months for it to be a profound and really effective study.

Chapter Two

When and How

We can work on our objectives anytime and anywhere.

We carry that computer, our mind, everywhere. The mind consumes more energy than any other muscle in the body. We need to be aware of it and decide that it is at our service.

Our highest goal is to control our thoughts. If you cannot control the internal dialogue and cannot guide it either, accept it.

Give it a lot of space to be as it is and then it will dissolve into nothingness.

Steps to Make to Reach the Goals

We have habits that are not really productive and we need to identify them. Eradicate useless actions. Avoid longing for what was negative and learn to replace it with new, useful and healthy habits.

For example, too much coffee, a sedentary lifestyle, eating outside of your schedule or an inadequate diet do not help our concentration.

Raise objectives that answer the question, **What for?** It is very important to stay motivated.

The characteristics of the objectives are that they must be general. They define what we will achieve; what obstacles I will encounter and what benefits I will achieve.

In order to be able to measure growth, the action plan needs to be concrete. Defining and visualizing each goal that we set increases our desire to reach the goal.

The goals are specific, strategies are elaborate, small steps are measurable and calculated. Many goals achieve the objectives.

In the planning, we will detail the repetitive actions, the priority actions, and the important actions.

We define the actions that we are going to protect, those that are not going to change no matter what happens.

The objectives have to motivate us to learn to do better every time. The motivation comes from the multiplication of beliefs by desire.

Part Two

Chapter Three

Massive Action Plan

Massive actions are the skills, knowledge, and resources that will lead us to the desired results.

Optimization of results, collecting ideas, consolidating ideas, selecting a concept and implementing the concept.

Repetitive Actions

Everyday activities that need to be converted into new habits. They include:

Make a wish board with images that you cut out from magazines, your own photos of happy moments or a make a collage. Look at the wish board whenever you can.

Read the list of objectives on paper, mobile or computer. Send yourself emails that will remind you that you are living the objective.

Listen to autosuggestion audio: Choose an audio that motivates and delights you.

Meditate: There are many meditation methods. Investigate which one is the most relaxing for you and practice it as many times as possible.

Priority actions

Get up early: time is finite. Tine is the greatest treasure if we get up at noon, we lose the whole morning. Apply your wake cycle and try to get up early. It helps if you go to bed at a reasonable time.

Social activity: A coffee with a friend or talking with family members provides us with emotional support in our daily life.

Physical activity: It is a priority to move the body; it needs to be in movement. Do it according to your possibilities and improve on the go. Going for a walk, for a run or swimming is essential. Exercises such as Pilates, yoga or hiking charge our determination with extra energy.

In the successful project, having a list of our strengths and weaknesses, a list of opportunities and threats will give us an overview of the path we are going to take. We can choose if we are willing to take it or not.

Important Actions

You should sometimes watch videos of people who have achieved success. I liked to watch the life of famous actors, presidents, scientists, athletes, who from nothing and almost without resources got to do great in their actions.

Watching the news 3 times a week is enough. We are not going to change the world by being soaked or submerged in the news, but it will indeed influence our positive energies. It is enough to just keep in touch with it.

Choose adventure movies, happy, funny ones and laugh a lot.

The Power of Self Discipline

It is necessary to have the "Vital Impulse" - the life energy that takes you out of the routine, the routine that our minds like so much.

For the dream seeker, leaving the comfort zone is to follow an impulse - that Vital Impulse that seeks to express itself.

It is the need that leads us to know more, to do more and to be more.

Have more things to use in order to learn and excel. The goal of enriching ourselves is to live more and to live better.

Desire is the power trying to manifest itself. That is looking for the most complete expression. The desire to have everything you can to express the best of each person, grow and help grow whoever comes in contact with you.

This is a challenge and we will go through it together.

Second Activity: Massive Action Plan

Positive thoughts calendar PLUS Massive Action

At this stage of the process, **WE COMBINE THE CALENDAR WITH THE MASSIVE ACTION**.

We are now able to determine the actions that generate constructive thoughts and actions that do not benefit us.

When making the calendar, we write the day, the action and what has been the predominant thought that has made us do them.

We determine which ones we will do every day, every month or every once in a while so that we have positive energy and we remain optimistic during this process.

Goal of the Month						
Actions + Results						
L	M	M	J	V	S	D
						1
2	3	4	5	6	7	8
9	10	11	12	13	14	15
16	17	18	19	20	21	22
23	24	25	26	27	28	29
30	31					

<u>Doing things in a certain way</u> implies going back to learning. Forget what you have learned until today and start again to see everything in a different way.

Determine if your dream is sporty, professional, artistic or personal - you will focus better:

1 Search for information on this topic through all the possible means, invest time and money in counseling in public, official or private centers.

2 Join the associations of workers, entrepreneurs, athletes or the groups that do these activities, and they excite them as much as they excite you. Participate, go to and meet up.

3 Search for all the information on the subjects that you are the most passionate about through written sources, videos or conferences.

Partner in crime: You can decide to do it alone or with the help of a friend, relative or a person with more positive energy than you.

You can also start alone and later have company; it is about choosing the best company so you do not abandon the actions that are effective.

Frustration or Failure

The feeling of failure exists and will always appear.

Some people suffer from it at the beginning; others suffer from it after a while.

It gets worse at night, during free days or a sudden memory activates it.

There are cases of frustration and very severe distress that may require medication prescribed by the attending physician. It should be interpreted as an aid but not as an already established solution. The medication is only useful for a period of time and then you need higher doses to achieve the same effect. It is a good time to do these activities while taking medication.

I got over it when I realized that there is no such thing as failure. I removed that word from my vocabulary.

Every time it wanted to arise in my mind I transformed it with these words: "I have learned".

Please remove the drama approach to life, remove the victimhood. It's not the end of the world, nobody kills you and you're not going to kill anyone. Just know that the present is the way it is and we are actively changing the course of it. The direction we were looking for was on the other side, it was in the opposite direction.

From each experience, you win or you learn. I promised myself that I will enjoy congratulating myself when I win and I will write what I had learned when I didn't win.

The mind encourages negative states because it is a habit, it is a custom. Today we are aware that we are re-educating our actions and the way we see events.

During anguish, people always talk about the same thing that only those people listen to, who have no other choice, like family and friends, who are as affected as we are.

All those actions will not take us where we want to go and that is having a wonderful, balanced, cheerful and happy life.

The Self-Analysis Test

Life Project

Whether it is because of great courage or great desperation, making the decision to radically change the direction of our current destiny is to overcome great obstacles.

The fear.

The brave are also afraid but there is an energy that drives them to overcome that fear. The energy of the "Illusion of making a dream come true".

The calling for a new life, a place far away from the circumstances that currently conspire against a full, complete and happy life, provoke different reactions in us.

There is no need for a crude or catastrophic reaction if we see ourselves very far from where we wish to be.

Answer the following questions in writing:

What drives us to do it?

What or who prevents us from it?

Do you have a company or are you going alone?

Why do you do it?

What factors do you count on? (Work, family or friends, savings, the possibility of personal development and development for the family)

Is returning to your state of frustration an option at this moment of time?

Have you set a time frame to assess your progress?

What will you do while searching for your goals?

What added value will it give to my daily life? Example: learn another language, meet new people, expand your business, get to know new cultures, travel and get to know more cities. It is proven that living every day as if it's the best gift of life is essential.

Reflect: How would you want to feel if you are in a new personal situation?

Imagine, how you are now and how will you be living the new life project?

In what period of time would you like to achieve that goal?

What value will it give to your life when you achieve the goal?

How will your family and friends see you when you achieve it?

It is essential to be clear about the objectives of such a radical project of change. If we write everything down in detail and read back everything written down, it will be easier to make the change, maintain our enthusiasm, energy, and motivation.

If you lose sight of the objectives, you lose your way and fall into what I have called the "Sweet Nothing".

Thoughts wander from one extreme to the other. Lost between two worlds, between two moods. Without doing anything here, without doing anything there. Living day to day, years passing by, getting older, emptier.

Transforming into a Successful Person entails:

Transforming all weaknesses into strengths

Opening doors that are closed right now

Using the differences that are surrounding you in your favor

The curiosity is always present in all aspects of your life

Knowing that failure is a part of success

If necessary, learn to fall causing the least possible damage, just like athletes do.

Get up with renewed energy, in search of more and better experiences.

Social Groups

Corporate bankruptcy doesn't mean the same thing in different societies.

For example, in the USA, if you say that you have suffered a bankruptcy, it sheds a positive image; they see you as a fighter who is gaining experience. However, among Latinos it is a negative image, you own nothing, you do not make ends meet and have worked for nothing.

Look at all the wonderful people, who are an example of the possibility of success. Even in moments of anguish you can be happy, it is a challenge, it is an experience, and we will overcome it together.

Successful people know that the support of a social group is essential. We are social beings but communities do not always support their members.

We must participate in a Proactive Community that helps with growth and is supportive. Positive and cheerful. One that organizes parties, trips, and enriching activities.

We create dreams on the bases of an objective reality. Reality is what everyone sees and agrees with. If you see that it is raining here and now, nobody will say otherwise, but if I say that the rain makes me feel happy, another person can say that their truth is that the rain makes them feel sad. In that case, what is really for one is not real for the other.

The objective truth is true for all, the subjective truth is personal.

The people around us can react to our decision to change in different ways. There will be people who accept the change well and there will be those, who do not. However, we are aware that you cannot win all the battles and that failures are a part of life.

Keep meeting people with a smile and do not pretend to be accepted by all. Look for new social relationships.

The Comfort Zone

With the topic of the comfort zone, I always choose the middle ground. Knowing what to choose, when is the right time to leave or stay, depends on each one of us.

Us, humans, can only focus on learning and growth if we are not worried about continuous changes.

Like a little plant, if we are continuously changing its place, its roots will never grow. The best thing is to leave the plant in one spot as soon as you have found the right soil, to make it grow healthy and strong.

Like a plant, children and people, in general, grow, when they are in their comfort zone. During the moments of growth, we need to be in the "safety zone". It is also necessary for our well-being to relax and remain still.

Calculated Crisis

The calculated changes help you feel stability when facing unfamiliar situations. We know that winter will come and we are prepared for it with proper clothing and adequate housing.

In the lives of successful people, the unknown will appear every day. We are much bigger than any problem because we are the solution.

This guide will help you just like a map; it shows us the way to identifying the challenges you must face alone and the ones you must face with the support of professionals, experts, friends or a loved one at home and so you are not alone.

Recognize the crisis as the opportunity for something better to enter your life. The crisis forces you to challenge your intelligence and improve. It is important to be constant even if you go slowly.

Know when to act and when to wait. The nature of situations sometimes solves itself if you give it time and space for it to do so. Act, wait for deadlines to be met and see what happens.

It is also well known that in times of crisis we speak without considering the damage we can do.

In a crisis, there are people who suffer in silence and others that seek to speak with malice, damaging everything that is close to them with sarcastic comments. We think that it is the end of our world and we don't see the needs of people around us, but instead how we can benefit from them.

The world is not over, it will continue as it always has after other crises we have gone through as children, adolescents or young adults.

Chapter 4

The Contrast Technique

At this point in our training, we are able to see our positive and negative thoughts, we see how our mind works and we know what our virtues and our shortcomings are.

It is necessary to focus our thinking on what we want in order to remove focus from what we do not want.

One technique that I recommend especially in this circumstance is "the contrast technique". It is easier to make a list of what we do not want than a list of what we do want.

You think about what you do not want but you write down the exact opposite. We leave the space for the title, once we have finished the list, we write the title:

"Yes, I want it"

This is who I am and I am willing to die for it.

Today, I know who I am, I know what I believe in and that is all I need to know. By believing we remain focused.

You have dreams, protect them.

The universe conspires to help you make it happen.

Technique to Clone Success Mentors

There are people who inspire us. Masters in doing and having what we aspire to have and do.

Study their work, look at their path, listen to their advice on how they got to that point – all that makes it easier.

In a focused, constant and targeted way we can move forward and make the leap towards our objectives.

It is wise to use your existing path so that you do not have to start from scratch. Let your ten be the zero, from where we start our project.

For my technique, doing what other people did to achieve or to get to the point where I would like to get, saved me a lot of energy and allowed me to continue with my activities.

1_ Discover what you are passionate about a sport, an activity, a craft, a business, a job. A craft that you like, identify with and that gives you possibilities. A profitable business with a future. A job, unlike employment, allows your personal growth. Employment is a routine and does not support growth.

2 _Total commitment to learning. Choose a teacher and learn with them for as long as necessary. A segment of time, a weekend, a week, a month or a year.

3 _Take distance. The neurons accommodate new information, new nervous circuits and return to total commitment to learning.

4_ Repetition with space - we let the brain adapt to the new learning system like the Zen master. Back to the massive action.

Let's be humble in these times, we will always learn better.

Being humble must always be present in our minds and hearts to be willing to learn from our teachers even the things that we should not be doing, both positive and negative.

Being stubborn can be a virtue or vice, depending on if it brings us closer to or away from success. The continuous assessment of where we have been and where we are today allows us to draw our conclusions.

Focus

It is advisable to put the focus on the following areas: Money, Relationships, Physical, mental and spiritual health. The path that is effective in motivating and precise.

1_ Clarity is fundamental: clarity is power. What I'm going to mold, what I want and why I'm going to do it.

2 _Quality Information: The best path, the best strategy and the strength of the team.

3 _Action: Move. A massive action is advisable. Every day act focused, be focused.

Equation of Results

It is necessary sometimes to stop the path to summarize what has been learned. New thoughts are generated and the thoughts that affect us the most are repeated.

World outside (Living the Thought)

We are subjected to impulses of life seeking to express themselves. It always leads us to know more, to do more and to be more for all this we must have more to use, more to learn and more to constantly improve.

Inner World (Internal Dialogue). The present state and the desired state. Pay attention: What do I say? Think? What do I answer to myself?

Ancient beliefs. Lies we believe.

Thoughts and words that provoke results. We must get rid of the pre-programming from the past. Choose to work with people who have your vibration and also want to improve. Progress - like any other human being, you want to grow. If it's done as a team, the effect multiplies.

With the will to think in a certain way and do things in a certain way will give us the result we want to replicate.

The hardest work is "Thinking the Truth" as it is inside of us, independently of how the present reality looks like.

Analyze and See Your Internal Dialogue

The internal dialogue is continuous. You have to redirect the dialogue towards what you want to feel and how you want to feel.

Thoughts of something being present or thoughts of something lacking.

What do you hear? Point it out because those are the deepest subconscious beliefs.

Pay attention - What do you say to yourself?

Note down what you repeat to yourself throughout the day.

Thoughts of Having Something

I see the opportunity, I learn how to do it, new skills emerge, new personal relationships. Challenges appear new challenges that I pass. I will ask the teacher what he does in order to have what he has. How he has achieved it. Feel that everything is closer.

Thoughts of Missing Something

I do not accept the lack of anything, no thanks. No thanks, today I do not want that. I do not accept negative teachers. They have an internal dialogue that is not mine. The focus of the loser is their focus, not mine. It is important to leave the whole thought process of lack. I am aware of what I have been telling myself. I forgive myself and I promise tomorrow, there will be less of a lack and more of having.

The Final Result

You can anticipate the final result by listening to the phrases you say. Where do your phrases point?

If you think about losing weight, you must have been fat before. You should think about: Being thin or Being a thin person.

If you think about getting healthy before you got sick more. You should think about: Being healthy or Being a healthy person.

If you think about work, you will work more. You should think about: Being abundant or Being an abundant person.

Generate Sources of Revenue

The bank does not accept love as a form of payment and the couple does not accept money as a form of love.

Money is important as a means of energy exchange necessary to live. Paying for proper nutrition and maintaining the family is essential to achieve fullness.

Having money to cover our needs reduces anxiety, decreases the feeling of something missing and the lack.

Time-Money Ratio

If you dedicate time to an activity, the skill improves – this goes for any aspect of your life. In the case of money, the more you think about it, the less you have.

It is a contradiction that can be solved by educating the constructive thought to focus on the presence of it and not on its lack. Think about how we will feel when we are without the worry of lack.

It is a very hard job to constantly keep your thoughts in a positive and balanced state. More so if the current reality is the opposite of what is desired.

Maintaining the thought of abundance, of health is only achieved if the mind is trained for it.

Reticular Activating System (RAS): if you activate the brain correctly, you will see all the ways to win.

You will know how to focus on the tools the right way and quickly detect opportunities. I will be attentive to new skills in order to increase their abilities.

Unconscious habits are like a mental virus. If you do not control your thoughts, you will not control anything else.

Having control over your thoughts allows us to live an idea. To live the thought. Blocking mentally everything that is not contributing to that Idea. Doubt and fear are recognized and discarded from thoughts.

Do not listen, do not see, do not share anything that is contrary to that idea. We will meet with complementary people, vibrating at the same frequency. We create a vibratory bubble together.

Practice focused repetition and also spacing. I give my brain time to familiarize myself with the new idea and I return to the repetitive thinking with full strength.

As a gymnast, there are periods of muscle training, of contraction and periods of stretching, relaxation.

I am giving my subconscious a new mental map; I program it again with "new beliefs".

I have to be the right person to be able to see opportunities when they arise. I will develop a sense that I had not developed before, to enhance my life.

At this point in our training, we are able to see our positive and negative thoughts, we see how our mind works and we know what our virtues and our shortcomings are.

It is necessary to focus the thought on what we want so that we remove focus from what we do not want.

One technique that I recommend especially in this circumstance is the contrast technique. It's easier to make a list of what we do not want than a list of what we do want.

Part Three

Chapter 5

More Massive Action

I put myself into action once I have clear objectives and the right beliefs:

1_ List 10 actions for success you can do in your projects you are busy with right now: for example, I have made a list of my knowledge in ..., experience in ..., I am learning ..., I like to do ....

2_ Overcoming the level of discomfort: acting even in adverse moments, against the opinion of our loved, implies a great willpower. Mistakes are transformed into doubts and fear of losing. Moving slowly and safely is also a way of overcoming it.

3_ Resolution Time: there are actions that need your time. Even if we give more intensity to a project, it will not speed it up and that we have to respect it. If a pregnancy takes 9 months, it is appropriate to wait it out. Some successes are a matter of time.

4_ Being the right person: the choice of the path you take, the right moment and even the team needed (lawyers, advisors, advisers, economists ...), everything has to be correct. Having the group that's right for you has a multiplying effect.

5_ If I can: when leaving your house, look carefully at all the opportunities that may arise in a conversation, in a course, during a walk or an exchange of information. Every day we have to set goals, even if the goal may be to rest.

Lifestyle

Life is simple, it is not necessary to complicate it. There are people who have the habit of complicating the simplest of things, creating problems where there are none.

Assess where you are on the road and re-calculate the arrival at the finish line. If it is necessary to make corrections to improve the result, they are made without a delay.

I also advise you to point out the small steps that we achieved, which brings us closer to the goal.

Personal Training

After having established the goals, observe your motivations and be aware of personal limitations you have with the activities.

Calculate the hours you dedicate daily to these activities. Making an activity calendar gets us organized, thus, we do not waste our efforts and we can manage the limited amount of energy we have.

Being aware that the day has only so many hours and that our body has a circadian rhythm will help us go down the stream. It is good to enjoy the path to success, avoiding abandonment, not losing motivation or enthusiasm when the time comes to the sweet or not so sweet waiting.

The Question of Attitude

The attitude of the champions is to take charge of their own life. It is not to look for guilt but rather to focus on solutions and not on the problem. Creating a habit of positive thinking, transforming ourselves into a successful person, in order to succeed. The right order is "to Believe is to See". I must believe that I am a successful person now so I am one tomorrow too. I am aware that the obstacles are bigger in my head than in reality.

Intensity

If you apply a lot of intensity into actions, you may not reach your goal. Here we come back to the example with the athlete: if you overdo it with the intensity, you can cause yourself muscle injuries that will make you stop temporarily or permanently.

Learning from Eastern Teachers

Eastern teachers have a way of doing and not doing things. The brain must be awarded the time of resilience when it gets used to the acquired knowledge. The body needs time to get used to new physical activity, the muscles need to rest. The head needs to rest too; it's just like cultivating fields.

Resilience Period

A successful person knows that the time of resilience and rest is the time when they are assimilating to new information.

In order to resume the action, it is a conscious and relaxing distraction that is also in line with the circadian rhythm.

The action is overrated. When we are working on the Life Project, being a bit bored can come very useful.

Having time to do nothing causes the brain, which is a muscle, to take a break. Savoring life means enjoying it when it is the right time.

This works for me: going to the countryside, going to the movies, meeting friends and carefully listening to other people and their lives. Changing the usual spots and rhythm helps with seeing our own experiences from a different perspective.

Going away, getting bored and taking a break is as important as taking action. In cases like these, the doubts get clarified from a distance and not by being submerged in the problems.

We can have clear objectives, do the right activities but the greater difference would be achieved with this one ingredient.

I consider the periods of relaxation to be very important in the overall development of this method. Being able to do it efficiently and recognizing the benefits helps the final result of the personal project.

Training Team

Reconsider your complete path again. See where you are on the mental map and if there are any small adjustments to make.

It is time to make all the corrections that are necessary.

One of the important aspects is the choice of the team, partner or partners in order to realize the project.

The actions and the story of life speak more than a thousand words. We must choose people more successful than us, people, who have reached the goals we want to reach or have the knowledge and hope to reach them.

It would be thoughtless to choose a team without knowing the end goal. Choosing a losing team, a demotivated team, a vague partner with no aspirations is the same as failing before you even start.

There are times when we should apply the phrase, "it's better to be on your own than in bad company".

While choosing the person, we can consider learning from them until we reach the next stage of our development and after that, each one of us continues with the path that we have chosen, without any resentment. We are all different; we know that everyone has their expectations and dreams. As Aristotle said, every person is a small world.

Tools

Making a list of the tools, mediums, techniques or equipment necessary to correctly develop the daily work is an aspect that we cannot ignore.

I consider tools to be such as the vehicle, the location, advertising, media, clothing, computer, knowledge, contacts, teachers, everything that adds value to the project, including your foresight.

Everything that does not add to it stays out - it obstructs it. All tools that are obsolete, or they do not benefit the project in any way, must be removed.

The tools wear out; we must observe them continuously to replace them when necessary.

Assessment of the Present State

It's important to review our endeavors every 21 days.

Be objective and write down each small achievement or what you have not achieved - this will give you the necessary information to efficiently and quickly reach your goals.

This way, you will be able to rethink the goals, the tools and recalculate the time, costs and benefits of the project. Making a decision in time can be the difference between success and losing the course of events.

Listen to the Signs

Some call it intuition, others hunch. Do not listen to the mind.

The signs are coincidences that indicate when something is stuck and when it is facilitated. It seems that what has to happen is facilitated, and what does not have to happen is interferes. Example: when you want to talk to someone with the reason of telling them things you should not be telling them in a reactive manner, the signs will cause that it will be difficult for you to reach the person. The experience shows me that everything gets worse. The pit gets deeper.

Follow the signs, which many people call "Flow".

Mental thoughts are preconditioned by our past memories, by wanting to protect ourselves from real dangers and also from the imaginary dangers that will never happen but in our mind, they are very real.

The mind must be used as another muscle of the body at the service of our will, not the other way around. We must train our thoughts and be aware of the constructive and destructive ones.

All people have a cellular memory; we all have thoughts and genetic information inherited from our family that can be either favorable or unfavorable for the success of the project we have chosen to pursue.

The power of success has to help us identify the differences and select which thoughts we want to keep in our minds.

Return to Action

When you have regained strength, clarified your thoughts and rested as long as necessary, it is time to return to action.

With renewed energies, we return with an open mind and we begin to see what was once invisible.

Ideally, get up early, take advantage of those 4 hours in the morning, do the daily chores and then spend 4 hours in the afternoon or evening on activities pertaining to your project.

There are people who work other jobs so they can only devote 2 or 4 hours to the project. If that is the case for you, the most convenient would be to devote time to it during weekends or holidays.

Different Time

Just as the weather can be destructive for the crops, the feeling of fear is an aspect that can work against the project.

We can choose to be positive and know that everything takes its natural time to develop or we can choose to be negative, decide that it takes too long and that it is time to quit.

The mental states within us can limit us or can make us free. Anguish, anxiety, and despair are paralyzing the action.

These are some of the consequences when we negatively assess the time factor.

It is as if someone was banging on the door to enter your house. Would you open it? Being softer is better.

The time remains the same; with delicacy the results are different. Even many successful people confessed that success came, when they least expected it or when they were distracted by other activities.

By removing pressure from a target, it starts to develop with natural efficiency.

A matter of time is not the same as a matter of correcting the actions taken. Differentiate it well.

As I said, the pregnancy takes 9 months, a university career lasts a while, physical preparation for an athlete too. The business objective needs a certain time, which we calculate according to what we discussed with the people around us. We will analyze if the actions are correct, if the method is correct or if we have the right tools because it is important to reach the goals.

The times like having fear are the aspects that can hinder the project.

Continuous Evaluation

It is very important to stop after a period of time and evaluate the path traveled, where we are and where we are going. We must evaluate the methods, the tools and the equipment used. Perhaps, when we started the journey, everything was right, but after a while, we should review it.

We must ask the right questions; does this help me or hinder me? Does it add or take away? Does it give me value or lack?

These are the questions that we can only answer with objective and subjective data.

There are moments in which we are very submerged and we do not see things clearly. We see the tree but not the forest. We need clarity of thought to analyze facts, comparing them to what our teachers and mentors did.

Each teacher has his own book, but a small difference can make a big difference.

Maintaining a pure spirit helps to achieve the expected results. I defend the idea or the way of acting of each person. There are those who achieved great things because they ignored the difficulty of achieving them. They did not know if someone had done it before.

The law must always be respected, the rules are there to be broken and the wise ones know the difference.

When we copy other people, we are only their reflection. Creating our own reflection respecting the law and creating new rules is wonderful.

Objectives achieved after 3 – 6 – 9 Months

Some recommend doing an assessment 3 months after starting the program. I do the assessment at 6 or 9 months checkpoint; my times are different. It generally takes three months to begin to see the results.

We make a list of the objectives achieved at work, with family, health or training. We also make a list of actions that were effective, of the ones that did not make a difference and ones that impacted the project negatively.

We reprogram the action plan and specify the objectives that we wish to achieve in the period of the next 6-months. This also includes what is expected from each team member.

The strategies must be defined. Everyone must have a written plan and mental manual of their duties, rules, and objectives. A defined economic plan of payments, savings and capital management for the project.

It is very useful to have a list of new actions.

Measurement of results allows us to make an assessment of the cause and effect. Record the actions that are working and eliminate those that do not work.

We must be proactive. Do not force actions against the stream.

Plan of Work

Redo the work plan and adapt it to the reality of the current moment.

For example, you had planned to raise the rent of the beach apartment but the economic crisis has lowered the demand. Reevaluating the market again allowed me to know what I could rent it for and the apartment was rented all summer long - unlike apartments of other owners, who did not adapt to the situation, and their apartments stayed empty.

Maintaining focus, being persistent, systematic and motivated gives us security when making decisions. We have the absolute confidence that doing what must be done will win the race in the background.

The person who starts a life project is never the same person when they finish it. There are always changes, something is always left behind, we stop being who we once were, to become different people. The best version of us can arise.

When the results are within the expected parameters, everything is fine. The problem is when the results are not the desired ones. Staying centered, against the negative internal dialogue that generates itself, helps us to stay focused.

That's when you have to be brave so the best version of you can come through.

New Functioning of Mental Processes

Controlling Obsessive Thoughts

Laughing about problems is a simple and wonderful therapy. The scratched disc of repetitive thoughts only shows us how crazy a person can become in certain situations.

Listening to music, watching movies or having other projects helps distract the mind. Tremendous, fatalistic thoughts distort the true importance of events. What is the worst that can happen? Is it deadly? Is your life at risk?

Detecting obsessive thinking and writing it down is a form of visualization. Also, wearing a reminder bracelet keeps us present at the current time, helping to interrupt the mental conversation.

The non-important obsessions or thoughts can be easily fought, "I'll think about that tomorrow" is the best therapy to achieve it.

Knowing How to Fall

Winning is very satisfying but nobody likes to lose.

Successful people know that losing is a part of learning and moving forward. You really fail when you abandon the life project. That's when you have chosen to feel unsuccessful.

When we play sports, they teach us that knowing how to fall is important to avoid serious injuries. When you have fallen in other projects, you have the experience of knowing when you are sliding smoothly and when you are definitely going down.

At that time, you can take urgent action to avoid falling and make the fall smoother.

Third Activity: Comparative Table

There are people with the feeling of failure so strong that they do not realize when they have already won.

Technique of evaluation of results

Exercises to Increase Trust

Rating Technique for Three to Six Months

We review the calendars we made in the last months. We review the objectives achieved and those that we have not reached yet.

We make a list

Recall…

Why did I decide to do it?

What did I decide to do?

Am I reaching the objective goals?

Am I reaching the subjective goals?

Being on the Path of Success

Real blocks. External blocks.

Personal blocks. The beliefs. Constructive or destructive family memory.

What do you?

What do you see?

What do they say?

What do I want?

When do I want it?

How many times do I want it?

What will I do with success?

Who will benefit from it?

How am I going to feel?

Self-motivate, Reasons for Action.

Self-illusion, Art of delusion.

For this reason, and because we need to motivate ourselves for the next challenge, we have to do the assessment test.

Strengthen self-confidence. Look in the mirror and see your worth as it is.

Do not continually judge everything that happens.

Do not be continuously alert for possible threats.

Stop controlling. The only things we can control are the thoughts and sometimes not even them.

Healthy relationships, respect, admiration.

If you do not like how things are, do not argue. Send them away from your life.

The biggest percentage of anguish is fantasy and fear. Do not let it control you. Relax, Live, Enjoy.

Anxiety clouds perception and the actual proportion of events.

Presumption is not certainty. Time and commitment to the objectives will tell the truth.

Take care of your thoughts; they are mental stories that generate anxiety, anguish, and despair.

Living day to day, step by step makes up life.

Be a spectator. What are the dominant thoughts you have right now?

Look with the eyes of justice; differentiate the actions from the events.

Define success; our own approval is more important than that of others.

Accept the best outcomes for yourself, because you deserve them.

Our principles, our deeply engraved truths do not change, but our understanding of them does.

Project:	Objectives of then.	People involved.	The obstacles I overcame.	The successes.	What I have learnt.
Point A Childhood:					
Point B Youth:					
Point C From 21 years old onwards:					
Point D					
Point E					

It motivates us to write down the objectives we had in past years, a list of what we learned, the obstacles we have overcome, the successes we had and the people who were involved.

Auto boycott

Remember that everything the mind says while having an anxiety attack is a lie. Do not believe it, it's deceiving you. It acts according to what it learned in the past. It's trying to protect you from ghosts. It tries to repeat the stories of your life that it already knows.

You should always pay more attention to the signs than to your mind.

Blaming is a way of manipulation. Self-reproaches, rigid thoughts, fixation on negative things.

In that moment of anxiety, it is best to meditate in silence and solitude.

The social group from your past will act just like your mind with cliché obsoletes, you can avoid venting to those people, the same as with your mind. You have to get out of the vicious circles.

Associate with more positive and successful people.

People do not recognize me for what I am but for how they feel when they are with me.

Concerns limit the visual field.

To win against you is the most powerful triumph that can be achieved in life.

The mind that is used the right way, the successful mind, must make a corrective revision upon making a mistake. Learn the lesson, forget the details and move on.

Focus on what is worth it

Do not waste your time on difficult people. An envious person will never help you, they will always hold a grudge, on the other hand, a detached person will always look for reasons to admire.

"I am the one who makes commands", I say to my mind and I commit to being successful.

Valuing my personal charm by looking in the mirror makes me look more beautiful.

Luck can happen, but the success we have to build. Luck depends on a chance, success depends on us.

Do you want to start again another way to success or not?

What is the model of life that makes the success concrete?

What's the difference between what you want and what you need?

Having the tests done, we must study the results.

For one, two, five, seven to ten years.

Make a comparative picture of your life.

After how years there is a significant change in your life?

How long does it take to have a new major change? If we establish our cycles we will have the best material to observe our own life.

Our life does not depend on spring, summer, autumn or winter, without seeing it as something positive or negative.

We will see how it is without being surprised by it.

Example of a Comparative Table

Year – Objectives	How long did it take until you achieved it?	Why did you do it?	Who helped you?	Short-term results?	Long-term results?
1980 - Degree					
1983 - Car					
1990 - Work					
1992 - House					
1997 - Trip					

Chapter 6

Living with the Enemy

We have all the freedom to remain asleep. When I was in the depths of my anguish I thought about what it would be like to die. That everything would end here and now. Nobody dies when they want to but when they should. Until that moment comes, we can choose to be what I have called "the living dead."

People who seem alive but have a heart of stone and their eyes are glass. They do not feel the pain of others, they do not realize the suffering they are capable of causing in other people.

Insensitive people walk the world breaking hearts.

They do not care what happens around them. They are the center of the universe and everything must revolve around them.

It does not occur to them to think about what they can do to help the world; they only focus on what the world does for them.

They know how to take advantage of situations, of each place and even of people.

Everything is a source of pain. They have a great ability to transform what happens in their life into suffering. They use their imagination in a negative way.

The people around them do not have the slightest possibility to give them joy, because these people transform everything into their personal meaning. But of course, with crystal eyes, because they are the first to cry for the least mean sentence people tell them.

Remember: The tree that has flowers lives from its roots. What nourishes its roots?

Just listen to the heart. Do you know the feeling that it has?

Now, how would you feel if you had to live the rest of your life as it is today? How would you feel about change?

You can always go back to the current situation. Changing life is a right, not an obligation.

When we return to anguish and frustration, everything looks different, because the person who returns is never the same as the person who has left.

Unpleasant Moments

If you have reached this chapter and done all the homework, this chapter is not for you.

If, on the contrary, you have arrived at this chapter and you have not done any of the calendars or tests, if you have started and you have not finished or if you have only read the book, without putting any action in, I will give you the last tool, a guide, if you still want to change your life.

This tool is very simple and fits this moment.

Every time you have an unpleasant moment during the day, no matter how small, describe it. We will indicate it by means of an exercise. We have to study our behavior so we can help ourselves.

The exercise consists of taking a notebook with you and noting down:

Situation: Day, Time, Where are you, With whom and what has happened.

I think: You should note down what you think at that unpleasant moment. Example: I'm stupid, I can't do anything right, ..)

I feel: You need to write down what emotion it gives you. Give it a name (fear, loneliness, sadness, guilt, ...)

Physical Sensation: Note down if your chest hurts, your tension goes up, you can't breathe well, you want to cry)

What do I do: Describe what action you take. You close up, go out, drink, take pills.

Make your life a valuable experience. We get rich when we reach the objectives but also when we do not reach them.

We have to be coherent between what we think, do and say. In this way, there will be no contradictions that increase anxiety and anguish.

We can be our worst enemy. Many times we set our limits and obstacles ourselves. There is no time limit for success. There are many known cases of people becoming successful in retirement.

It only depends on you if your life is worth living, it depends on the decisions we make.

Situation What happened?	Thought	Feeling	Physical sensation	What do I do
Point A				
Point B				
Point C				
Point D				
Point E				

Meditation Techniques

Meditation is a great help to recover inner peace during times of great anguish. Silence the voice of thoughts and recover part of the essence of yourself.

We must be aware of the importance of meditating. It is difficult to stop in the world as fast as the one we in.

There are many benefits of meditation, some of them are the following:

It decreases stress.

It decreases anxiety levels.

It helps to reflect on one's own experience.

It increases your self-awareness.

It has positive effects on general health.

It improves attention and concentration capacity.

It improves interpersonal relationships.

It reduces painful symptoms because it increases pain tolerance.

As indicated by some studies, it can improve memory.

It helps to have an optimistic and positive attitude.

I studied and practiced many types of meditation. Buddhist meditation cultivates the mind so that the person who does this meditation finds himself in the reality of the now in order to "increase his understanding and wisdom". Meditation in yoga is not a religion or a belief; it is a series of simple techniques that make use of the mind, the senses and the body "to create a communication between them". There is mindfulness meditation, which consists of a set of exercises that the instructors or teachers organized in a sequence, as a more effective way to access the changes that may benefit us.

There are meditations you can do while you walk, meditation while sitting, meditation while we are in contact with nature, praying is also a way of meditating. There are meditations with sounds that are based on mantras or chakras, which are seven energy centers in the body.

Each person needs to experience conscious relaxation and apply the most effective method every day.

They are performed in the morning as soon as we wake up, in the evening and before sleep, at night. It should not last less than 15-20 minutes for it to be effective.

Personally, the meditation that gave me the most results were, in fact, a combination of several of them. In Mindfulness we usually use 5 types of meditations:

Breathing Awareness

Scanning of the body

Conscious yoga with flexibility exercises

Opening meditation in sitting position

Compassionate meditation

A scientific study supports it. Professors Bethany Kok and Tania Singer from the German Max Planck Institute, with more than 200 participants, evaluate four meditations (all except yoga) and compare the data of those who practice them for 3 months.

In spite of being different, all the meditative practices resulted on positive emotions within patients, more energy, more focus in the present and less distraction of thoughts, compared to when they have only started with the practice.

The benefits of each of the meditations are:

Conscious breathing: the practitioner maintains a sensitive observation of their respiratory process at the level of the nostrils, chest, and abdomen. They don't change the rhythm; they only feel that they are breathing.

Body scan: in this practice, you try to feel, progressively, each physical sensation of the body from one end to the other, such as heat-cold, humidity-dryness, tingling, vibrations and pain.

Meditation with attention to the thoughts: the thoughts are observed as they are passing without "merging" into them (staying hooked).

Meditation of compassion: it is a practice where visualization is also incorporated since we try to feel kindness and compassion for all those around us and for the beings of the universe in general.

To some extent, practicing meditation requires achieving a certain degree of concentration for a while and decreasing the distraction. When we achieve this, we reach a certain degree of calmness and that directly benefits our mood and attitude towards life. But here they seemed to end the similarities.

Certain benefits

Each meditation proved to have its own beneficial characteristics, even without the support of the others.

It happens that in the Mindfulness program, for example, to practice observing thoughts one first learns to observe the breath in order to focus the mind. Only after that one goes to observe the thoughts.

There is a new study that highlighted the progressiveness of this practice: each group practiced a type of meditation for 3 months and this is what the participants reported through questionnaires:

Breathing meditation: more focus and concentration. More calmness

Body scan: greater interoceptive awareness (body sensations) and decrease in negative thoughts of the past and future.

Observation of thoughts: maximum ability to observe and not merge with thoughts. Less mental activity

Compassion: greater development of thoughts, positive emotions and warmth in relation to others.

According to the researchers, each practice seems to create a distinctive mental environment, and the consequences of long-term practice must still be explored.

This study is really just part of a larger investigation called "Resource Project" (something like project resources). It examines how different meditations affect the brain structure, stress, and social behavior.

I recommend to practice it and choose the best one for every need.

Diseases and Emotional Meaning

The forms of medicine are evolving over time. If we go through history, we will see all the changes that society has achieved.

"Disease is the effort that nature makes to heal the man" Carl Gustav Jung.

Currently, there is a strong tendency to heal us more naturally without so many chemicals. We have new types of medicine that are making their way through.

One of the alternative medicines proposes to find the origin of the diseases or their emotional meaning in order to treat them. It's called Biodecoding. According to the Greeks, humans somatize everything that affects him.

The basis is that our body, mind, and soul are closely related. It studies the functioning of our unconscious mind and the impact that emotions have on our organism.

They say that every disease has an emotional origin, that is, it is caused by some kind of feeling that does not manifest itself as such, and that is why it is projected on the physical body. They support the belief that behind all symptoms there is an unresolved emotional conflict that is hidden behind an illness.

Disease occurs when there is no coherence between what we feel, do and say when there are contradictions and oppositions between the parts that make up our being.

A coherent person acts in accordance with his ideas and expressions. Our brain does not distinguish between real, symbolic, virtual or imaginary. For our mind everything is the same. Everything is real.

Faced with a situation of great emotional pressure, such as a layoff or a divorce, and remaining in the same social, economic and personal circumstances, the reactions of people can be very different:

Seeing the opportunity to change their lives and, instead of lamenting, they put themselves in action, look for a new way of life and even thank for the change.

Sinking into a well of fear, they are filled with anguish and won't stop wondering what they will do, how will they do it, if they want to get ahead now or how will their children eat?

Closing up, convinced that they won't be able to find anything at this moment due to their age and the real picture of the employment situation.

Observing these attitudes and the dynamic choice adopted by each type of individual, it is very likely that they will resort to the second or the third example, that they do not have a single name and they even may have a serious illness over the years. However, for the first type of person, it is not only easy to find a job, but they will also maintain their health.

The influence of emotions on our health is increasingly evident to the point that no medical professional denies it nowadays.

Cornered Brain

When we are in periods of crisis, the brain experiences the belief of being cornered by fear. It's impossible to react.

We are paralyzed in an unconscious way, in an attempt to find a solution. There are too many emotions that we feel that add to the not understanding that is within us.

When something surprises us at very high levels, the inability to react is a mechanism of self-defense. To recover the balance that has been suddenly plunged into chaos, we use this paralysis.

When we are destabilized, uncertainty comes right after the paralysis. We have to make decisions after a crisis. Weigh the situation in order to choose what action to take. There is an excess of distrust towards the outside world.

The person feels threatened and may react by fighting or fleeing. It explodes in excessive chaos.

Accompany the Friend

A person who experiences a crisis asks us for help even if they don't express it in words.

What we can do is to channel calmness, serenity and try to guide them towards a much calmer emotional state.

We must remind them that we are all free.

If something disturbs us, we have to change it. If the change is not possible, we must accept it and finally, if it is not possible to change or accept it, we must leave it. Leaving a situation that makes us imbalanced is the best choice.

From my personal experience I can say that if you help someone too much, it becomes useless. Helpless, he cannot fend for himself. In the economic, emotional or physical aspect, if they help us too much we become helpless.

If I resolve someone else's life, in a certain way I am telling them that they are incapable to take charge of their life. We have to help just enough so that they can help themselves the rest of the way.

Sometimes, being needed seems to satisfy the need of being recognized, for them to see us as generous, compassionate and committed. The great majority of the redeemers in history ended up being crucified by their followers. We all need to feel satisfied and have a sense of personal worth when we help others.

One thing is to reach out to the underdog so that he can rely on us in difficult times, and the other is to focus my self-esteem and personal worth trying to get my loved ones out of their emotional, existential and even economic problems.

A person with clear symptoms of emotional dependence feels that their well-being, emotional security or happiness depends on other people or on what they do, say or think about them.

In the end, by looking for ways to help others, without intending it, we help ourselves. The best way to get ahead is by helping others but always in a proper amount.

We have to gain experience. Only by doing the actions we learn. Doing a lot is not the same as doing it well. First, a lot is done and then you learn to do it well.

The Circumstances Change

A circumstance is an external factor that affects a specific person. A circumstance is a specific situation that has certain qualities and characteristics.

Everything comes, everything happens and everything changes.

We have three choices when we face unpleasant circumstances:

Changing ourselves or what we dislike.

Accepting ourselves or what we dislike.

Leaving it, we abandon the thought because it does not make sense to continue with the obsession, leave work or leave the relationship or friendship, partner or whatever.

If we have to choose "to leave" we must be aware that we will go through stages of grief that are recognized by all who have suffered a loss.

Stage of denial: denying the reality of a loss helps cushion the blow and defers part of the pain caused. It is very helpful for our body because it allows us to change our mood and helps us not be so abrupt.

Stage of anger: the resentment that appears in this stage is the result of the frustration that comes from knowing that there was a loss. There is a strong sense of anger that is projected in all directions because we can't find a solution; we are looking for the person who was responsible for it.

Stage of the negotiation: we fantasize with the idea of reversing the process and look for strategies to make that possible. We imagine that we have gone back in time and nothing has happened. It is a short stage.

Stage of depression: it is not the same as depression that is considered a mental disorder. The present feels like a deep sense of emptiness. Deep sadness occurs and we have to live it through in the present.

Stage of acceptance: by learning to continue living in a different world, you accept the circumstances as they are now. We must actively reorganize the very ideas that make up our mental state. It is characterized by a lack of intense feelings and fatigue.

Adapting to Change

Recognizing and accepting changes are part of daily life.

We must control ourselves. However, some people are more resistant or have difficulty to adapt and take advantage of them, compared to an average person.

Knowing how to act in uncomfortable situations will allow us to put aside the emotional anguish. Prepare a small action plan on how to proceed with the change.

You must accept the changes and feelings that it caused us. Approaching other people and sharing our experiences, reactions, and emotions helps us to alleviate the tension that we can feel. We must maintain a positive attitude and be flexible.

Every human being has the ability to adapt to change, even if it takes more time than they thought. Do not expect to feel comfortable quickly; it may not be possible in the short term.

The ability to adapt means being flexible when things change. An adaptable person is one who is open to new ideas and concepts.

Similar Vibrations

Good and bad vibrations can be the cause of people's positive or negative behavior.

There are special people in the world who transmit positive energy, a special energy that makes them shine and that others perceive and appreciate because it makes them feel good and positive. They smile because they cannot help it; practically, the smile shines through their faces.

The positive energy is that magnet of vitality that you manage to project into your environment through a kind word and a smile. It is that magnet of force that flows from us when we manage to align the mind and heart with the kind side of life.

There are times when it seems that we are capable of moving mountains and others, were getting out of bed is a great feat. The key is in our personal energy, which allows us to get excited, to commit ourselves to what we do or simply, to feel good.

When we are exhausted, it is not always because of stress, but because we have not dedicated effort or time to recover energy.

The same happens with money: if we always withdraw and never deposit, we will have an unfavorable balance. Therefore, a disciplined attitude to find ways to recover is one of the best choices we can make if we want to feel good.

Relating to people who vibrate positive energies is fundamental to get better. If we do not choose the people and partner that we have around us well, they will take our energy and we can finish the day or start in the morning already exhausted.

Just as positive emotions such as calmness, challenge, commitment, optimism, and trust, improve our performance, negative ones such as frustration, impatience, sadness and fear gradually lead us to a disaster.

We need to take care of our energy, maintain it and, if we lose it, recover it – this is very important to lead a balanced and healthy life.

We live in our bodies. Analyze with sincerity how you can improve and find a simple way to make it come true. For example, listening to music (relieves obsessive and worrying thinking, generates changes in mental activity, moving from the rational left hemisphere to the intuitive right); with the body language acting as if you is already happy and living a full life makes you show externally what you want to feel in inside, being able to experience healthy emotions.

Work and Observe your mind, your internal dialogue, what do you say over and over, what do you say to the world? Identify what you do not like, and learn to change it with the techniques we have developed in this book.

The coherence between body, mind, and spirit is what will help us maintain and increase our personal energy. Meditation and the techniques of changing what we do not like, of accepting it or of leaving it, is the healthiest thing you can do for yourself.

Remember that everything that does not grow in nature, ages and dies. It dies mentally, professionally, as a couple or family member. We must deal with our growth, enrich our knowledge, and improve everything we like to do (cooking, sewing, sports, reading ...)

Talk with people who stimulate for you and be an apprentice you whole life. Acquire new experiences with openness and flexibility in order to recognize excellent people and great opportunities.

Neuronal reconditioning

A few years ago, scientists argued that a child at the time of birth has already a structured brain development and that basically this was preconditioned by the genetics. That is, the importance of early experiences and the environment in their development was not recognized.

Nowadays it is known that this is not the case, the first three years of life and especially the first one, is the most important for the future, in this time one should try to give the necessary stimulation for optimal development of the baby.

Two people are born, their brains can be considered "equal" structurally, however not functionally. The same elements are present, but the neuronal prolongations (dendrites) have not yet grown. It will be the environment, through timely and adequate stable experience, that will "wire" it and make it functional.

The nerve cells have the property of reorganizing their existing connections and of modifying the biochemical and physiological mechanisms involved in communication with other cells throughout life; which will affect learning and effective life. These changes will occur in critical periods of development where the stimulation should be given to have a greater arborization of the dendrites.

Now it is proven that the efficiency of this "wiring" is influenced by socio-environmental and economic factors.

Knowing this research is of utmost importance as we are going to reprogram our neural wiring with the techniques that we have developed in this book.

We know that the nervous system continues to develop even after birth, so our actions should be aimed at providing optimal stimulation (affective and effective) at key moments, change in our lives to maintain and optimize neuronal function.

Mental maturation continues beyond, a certain point will make the nervous system more efficient over time.

Symptoms of Neuronal Reconditioning

It is my duty to prevent that, when we are working on our mind, when we are creating new neuronal wiring, we experience emotional and physical symptoms.

The processes of understanding, feeling, perceiving, reasoning, planning, inferring, relating ... are carried out and/or mediated by the brain.

This organ organizes and supervises all the functions of the human organism and if we transform it voluntarily or involuntarily it provokes a series of reactions.

Consequences of neurological changes:

Migraine: the person experiences discomfort or pain localized in any part of the head that usually remits spontaneously or with the help of an analgesic.

Tension Headache: The sensation is that something squeezes the perimeter of the head. The oppressive pain occurs throughout the head. The treatment may require constant medication.

Muscle contraction: The muscles of the neck and scalp become tense or contract and can also cause headaches. Muscle contractions can be a response to stress, depression or anxiety.

Gastrointestinal Disorders: The gastrointestinal tract is highly innervated by the Autonomous Nervous System, a channel of physiological expression of emotions, making it one of the most frequent locations of psychosomatic disorders, changes in mood.

Insomnia: anxiety disorder causes difficulty in falling asleep or maintaining sleep.

Sleeping Well

The human beings and many other mammals spend a large part of the day sleeping. We spend a third of our lives asleep. Thus, the sleep pattern is one of the most important processes for correct functioning at a physical and psychological level.

We need to sleep. The processes that explain sleep are part of the sleep-wake cycle, the most important circadian rhythm. It lasts 24 hours and allows the body to recover or restore biochemical and psychological processes that have deteriorated during wakefulness.

While these regenerative processes take place, the body rests in order to be physically and mentally active during wakefulness. In a simplified way, we could say that we need to sleep in order to be awake.

In spite of the popular thought that the dream is a passive process and related to the "deactivation" of the mind, in reality, the brain presents a great activity while we sleep.

Specifically, the dream consists of two different states of neuronal activity: these are REM sleep and non-REM sleep.

REM (rapid eye movement) sleep occupies 20% of the total sleep time and usually occurs every 90 minutes. In this stage, the electrical activity of the central nervous system has intensity similar to that of the waking state, and there is an increase in heart rate and respiratory rate.

<u>Studies indicate that REM sleep is connected to memory and learning processes.</u>

As a consequence, being deprived of the REM phase makes it difficult to integrate new information learned in wakefulness and even prevents the adequate emotional management of important situations.

Non-REM sleep is composed of four phases that move us from a more superficial state of sleep to a deeper one. These periods allow regulating the mood, among other functions.

In stage 1 the transition from wakefulness to sleep occurs and the body muscles relax completely. Phase 2, which occupies 40% of total sleep, is the one that has a longer duration; in this state, the person can wake up with external stimuli of moderate intensity. From here we go to phases 3 and 4, in which the dream is deeper; it is during these sub-phases that nightmares usually happen.

Insomnia and sleep deprivation cause serious alterations in the body. In particular, they have a negative influence on attention and perception and increase the number of memory errors and irritability, which in turn favors the occurrence of feelings of anxiety and stress.

The functioning of the higher brain functions is altered; this interferes with cognitive performance so that when sleep deprivation is severe, carrying out daily tasks successfully becomes a feat.

At the brain level, sleep deprivation directly affects the prefrontal cortex, responsible for practical reasoning and logic, as well as working memory, that is, the active management of memory information during a short period. A lower activation of the temporal lobe, involved in language processing, has also been identified.

In this way, even understanding what others say and developing appropriate answers can be complex. It also worsens the activity of the thalamus, a subcortical structure involved in attention and alertness.

There are studies that relate sleep deprivation to psychosis, the spectrum of mental disorders where schizophrenia belongs. In this sense, they claim that the lack of sleep makes it difficult to manage emotional events from the proper perspective so that inappropriate responses are given to normal stimuli.

So far, Randy Gardner is the only person who has spent the most hours without sleep in a scientifically proven way, voluntarily and without using any type of stimulant. Specifically, he stayed awake for 264 hours, which is equivalent to 11 days.

During the period in which Gardner was without sleep, the researchers controlled several variables. The alterations began with changes in mood and being irritated. After days passed, delusions and visual hallucinations appeared, and the focus of the subject happened to be zero.

There are records that show that during the Second World War the Nazis used sleep deprivation as a method of torture. Science suggests, from the results of experiments with rats, that death occurs between 3 and 4 weeks after the onset of sleep deprivation.

After this brief journey about the implications of sleep on the organism and the negative repercussions of sleep deprivation, we can conclude that sleep is one of the most necessary processes for the proper functioning of the organism.

It is, therefore, necessary to give it importance and to follow good habits in the process of going to sleep; we call these routines "sleep hygiene". These are some of the most relevant examples:

Maintain a fixed schedule for bedtime and getting up.

Avoid naps longer than 30 minutes.

Do not stay in bed longer than you need to sleep.

Avoid copious meals before going to sleep; it is advisable to wait two hours after dinner.

Avoid doing activities in bed such as reading, watching television or listening to music.

Maintain a comfortable temperature in the room and wear baggy clothes like pajamas.

The effects they have on your body

One of the most widespread recommendations about sleep is to sleep about eight hours a night. This is supported by research that indicates that both those who sleep a lot and those who sleep little are more likely to suffer certain diseases and live less.

A person who sleeps a little enjoys less than 6 hours of sleep daily; while a person is considered to sleep too much is if they do it for more than 9 or 10 hours a day.

The importance of good sleep hygiene

Experts know that chronic lack of sleep, being deprived of one or two hours of sleep a day for a period of time, is linked to poor health. You do not have to spend days without sleep to suffer these negative effects.

One of the diseases that affect sleep is depression. It causes the total time asleep to shorten due to being up early, which is associated with the inability of the individual to go back to sleep; and anxiety disorder causes difficulty in falling asleep or maintaining sleep.

If you have trouble falling asleep or are interrupted and kept awake at night, you have the chance to act on it and fight the cause of it.

Anxiety

Scientists found a close link between anxiety and sleep disorders, which have increased dramatically

The technologies

The National Sleep Foundation conducted a new study among US citizens to find out if the use of technology is related to sleep disorders. The study determined that excessive use of technological devices misaligns the internal clock and alters the hormones that help to fall asleep; they interrupt it and cause fatigue. 43% of the respondents said that they rarely or never sleep well during the week and 60% reported sleeping problems all or almost every night.

It is necessary to lower the rhythm of the body in the last hours of the day as the use of any device will leave you excited. This will prevent you from falling asleep, or cause you to wake up tired.

Watch TV

In the study of the National Sleep Foundation, 95% of respondents acknowledged that they use some type of electronic device such as a television, computer, video game or cell phone a few nights a week before bedtime. 60% said that they do it almost every day, exposure to artificial light between dusk and bedtime at night suppresses the release of melatonin, the hormone that promotes sleep, it reinforces the state of alertness and causes changes in heart rate, making it more difficult to sleep, "said Charles Czeisler, Harvard Medical School.

Take work home

Taking work home and not separating from communication technologies is a recurring practice of executives, which affects their ability to sleep and the quality of rest. In Mexico, 1 in 10 people suffer from insomnia and 2 out of 10 have a smartphone, which they do not put away before sleep.

Experts advise respecting the time needed for recreation and rest. We have to put down limits because the sum of working hours and the lack of fun produce stress, and in the long run, our health will suffer, causing illnesses that we will have to face sooner or later.

Health problems

Disorders that can cause insomnia: diseases with chronic pain such as arthritis, headaches, asthma and heart failure, too active thyroid and gastrointestinal disorders, among others, according to the National Heart, Lung and Blood Institute.

Stress

Significant or prolonged stress and disturbances of emotional state cause insomnia. Trips and work schedules that alter sleep habits can also cause primary insomnia, a sleep disorder that is not due to any other medical problem.

Menopause

To relieve insomnia at this stage, the Cleveland Clinic advises: keep the bedroom cool to prevent night sweats, avoid using sleeping pills, exercise daily, avoid caffeine and alcohol at night, and eat cereal products and milk before going to bed or during the night.

Bad night habits

It may make you sleepless if you take a nap, exercise very close to bedtime, eat heavy meals, drink too much liquid or not always go to bed at the same time. The ideal is to get used to doing things that calm and relax you before going to sleep, like reading a book, listening to soft music or having a hot bath.

Coffee and alcohol

Caffeine is a very powerful stimulant that influences sleep. Coffee, tea, sodas, and chocolate contain it. You should avoid it 6 hours before going to sleep.

And the shots too: cause a lighter than normal sleep, which is less sustained

Sleeping pills

There are many prescription medications for sleep. The National Library of Medicine reports that some should be used for a short period and others are used for a longer time. The doctor should be consulted about the benefits and side effects of these pills: many cause discomfort or cause dependence that eventually causes insomnia.

Rest and relax

Lack of proper rest reduces the immune response of our body, lowers the defense and we may have a smaller resistance to colds. Reduces cognitive function, concentration and increases bad moods. It increases the risk of cardiovascular diseases, increases the risk of obesity and can also affect the control of glucose.

Physical exercise is essential to get more tired before sleep. Going for a walk, dancing or any physical activity helps us to reduce stress and tension

1) Learn to manage your time.

2) Find better ways to cope with stressful situations.

3) Take good care of yourself, try to get enough rest.

4) Eat well.

5) Do not smoke and limit alcohol.

6) Learn to say "no".

7) Express your emotions.

8) Ask for help from professionals.

Certain prescription or over-the-counter medications can disturb sleep. This problem can be easily solved by asking your doctor which ones will not affect your sleep quality and in any case, ask for an alternative, advises the National Heart, Lung and Blood Institute.

An effective option without taking medication is cognitive behavioral therapy, which involves talking to a therapist individually or in group sessions to discuss your ideas and feelings about sleep. The objective pursued by this therapy is to learn to relax and clear the mind.

Causes of Excessive Sleep

It refers to feeling abnormally sleepy during the day. People who are sleepy may fall asleep in inappropriate situations or times.

Excessive sleepiness during the day, without a known cause, can be a sign of a sleep disorder.

Depression, anxiety, stress, and boredom can contribute to excessive sleepiness; these conditions almost always cause fatigue and apathy.

Epilogue

Congratulations, you have achieved success.

The power of success is also in congratulating oneself, rewarding oneself, feeling success, living success, valuing achievements, goals achieved, fears conquered. Fear of heights, fear of falling, fear of not being able to lift the feet off the ground.

The path of having it is in line with learning how to maintain it. During The Road to Success, we will also learn how to stay there if you are a good student and you fulfilled each of the activities we have proposed in this book.

Make a list of all achievements. An objective and subjective list.

Detail 10 positive things that have been achieved in this project. Make a list of people who need to be thanked for their help, support, and companionship along the way.

A list of things that have been learned or improved.

Today, we know that the road to success teaches us how to maintain success and to continue to achieve personal success until the end of the day.

Remember that there is always time to have a coffee or a beer with a friend. Family and love are fundamental sources of energy and inspiration.

Putting the added value to each situation will make us more complete.

Do not tell anyone.
The silence

Cultivate the gift of contemplating life as a whole but from outside the mind. Silence is the absence of noises that prevent us from hearing the beauty of the sounds of life.

The testimony of other people makes us wise and intelligent. We only tell our experiences to the persons who listened when went through it, when we have already overcome it, accepted or achieved it.

When I went out to tell everyone about my experience, I had the impression that they looked at me like I was crazy.

I have decided to help only the ones who want to be helped. I only tell the ones who want to listen because experience has taught me that the other way is only a waste of my energy that is already limited. Throwing pearls at pigs does not benefit anyone.

I also keep in mind that silence is a great virtue. Only if you are quiet you can listen. In this way it is possible to listen to our hearts; our intuition always whispers, it does not scream. In silence, we listen to it.

Transform weaknesses into strengths.

It is a great virtue of humans to transform weaknesses into strengths. Know that it is part of a game and you can start over as many times as necessary until you achieve the goal, the success.

We all know that what does not kill us makes us stronger. It also happens that what does not kill us weakens us. In the career of success, what do you choose to think?

Does it weaken you or make you stronger?

Trust in your Potential

We have reached the end. You already have all the tools. Everything has prepared you to be here and have this opportunity. You have all the knowledge - it's time to trust your potential and launch yourself into the world.

Today you can illuminate the darkness.

What do you do with what happens to you? What do you do with what goes through your mind?

In a balanced person, the best refuge is oneself. Meditating is the recommended mental exercise to increase the power of success.

Are you aware when you are traveling the same way but with different names? Are you aware of the fact that you have not yet learned anything new and are in a loop of repeating the same story?

Dissociation in a person is to do one thing, say one thing and think something different. I am not that person. Being one is the healthiest and it's the path to success.

You know to what extent you should spend without going over the poverty line.

Did you know that even to go bankrupt, to close a business you have to have money? I found out when it happened to me that I had to close down for lack of money and had to pay what I could not.

Which point can you reach?

When should the direction of the goals be changed?

Can you lower your head, put aside your pride, silence your ego and take another path?

Why are there people who seem to work a lot and do not have a penny and why are there people who do not seem to work and are millionaires? Easy, because the latter ones are in their life project. They are synchronized with their being. They do, they think and they are the same.

Ask the right questions: Did you like it, did you have fun, what did you enjoy the most, what did you learn?

Today I am with you, we are doing it together.

There are people, who are so pessimistic that they do not realize that they have triumphed. Do not be like them.

When you reach the goals, celebrate it, celebrate it and feel the Power of Success.

We will know each other by our success.

Because after all, we have to ask the question my father asked me:

"Daughter when 100 years pass is this going to matter?" and always ends by saying ...

"Because after all, this will also pass."

Thanks

I decided to write this book when a person dear to me, Javier, had to go through the experience of losing his family business, a divorce, a huge debt and start his life again at 45 years old.

I remember the challenge when I had to relive the anguish of starting life from scratch for the second time and feeling lost but this time as an observer.

Seeing how a loved one suffers without being able to intervene is a test. A challenge.

Knowing that if I help too much it won't benefit anything, I only postpone something that the person must overcome on their own.

Knowing that I could fall back into the depression I had overcome; because in despair, the other person does not see that we can drag others into the mud and sink altogether.

I had to have enough criteria to know how far my strength could go, when I should just stay close and when to distance myself.

At that moment I saw him suffer and I told him: "You must be calm, be positive, feel lucky you are alive".

He asked me: "It's okay, you're right but how is it done? How do you do it? Where do you buy that?

They tell you what to do but nobody tells you how to do it. The one who has overcome a crisis, such as you, does not explain how to do it ".

He was very right. I had already overcome the worst storm of my life and I did not remember how I had accomplished it.

It took me a year to compile all my notes and notes to find the steps of how I had achieved it.

I had everything noted down.

Today I feel the need to pass on my experience and help others achieve their successes. I give you this book to share my experience.

The experience has given me the tools to help everyone who is going through or overcoming a personal crisis.

Tell them what we did.

Today I can confirm that success in life is the best remedy for anxiety, anguish and lack of personal appreciation.

My desire to help without intervening in the natural awakening of each person has been my motivation to write this book.

Being close, being at his side, without intervening not to hinder his growth.

My challenge was not to fall into contagious frustration. Get to agree with yourself.

My sincere thanks to my loved ones because they are my inspiration and are my continuous motivation.